Nehemiah Matson

Beyond the Atlantic

Eleven months' Tour in Europe, Egypt and Palestine

Nehemiah Matson

Beyond the Atlantic
Eleven months' Tour in Europe, Egypt and Palestine

ISBN/EAN: 9783337235895

Printed in Europe, USA, Canada, Australia, Japan

Cover: Foto ©Andreas Hilbeck / pixelio.de

More available books at **www.hansebooks.com**

BEYOND THE ATLANTIC,

OR

ELEVEN MONTHS TOUR

IN

EUROPE, EGYPT AND PALESTINE,

WITH ILLUSTRATIONS.

By N. MATSON.

PRINCETON, ILLINOIS:
REPUBLICAN JOB PRINTING ESTABLISHMENT.
1870.

PREFACE.

Of late, books of travel have been increasing at a rapid rate, and the public taste for that kind of reading has proportionately increased. Each succeeding traveler views things in a different light, being inspired with new ideas, thereby furnishing the reader with some important facts which have been overlooked by his predecessors.

These pages were written from notes taken among the scenes which they describe, and only treat of objects coming under the writer's own observation. It will be found to consist principally of short descriptions of places; and facts alone are given, without the opinions or impressions of the writer, leaving the readers to draw their own conclusions. This work will be found to differ from other books of travel, inasmuch as it is composed of sketches, under separate heads. Each article is conclusive in itself, and can be read without doing injustice to other parts of the chapter. At the same time, each connects with the others, so as to form a continuous chain.

These sketches embrace the observations made during an eleven months tour, and over a distance of more than twenty-five thousand miles; consequently the description of places and things, must necessarily be brief. This could not be otherwise, without extending these pages far beyond their present limits, thereby making the enterprise pecuniarily a hazardous one.

The public will bear in mind, that this work makes no claim as a literary production, and is simply designed to give a plain statement of facts. It is hoped that the reader will view it from this standpoint, without taking exceptions to the plainness of the style in which these facts are presented.

N. MATSON.

Princeton, February 1st, 1870.

CONTENTS.

viii

ix

CHAPTER I.

On the fourth day of March, 1868, I left New York on the steamship Caledonia, bound for Glasgow, Scotland. The passage, although a rough one, was void of any incident worthy of note until the twelfth day, when we came in sight of the mountains which adorn the north-west coast of Ireland Off the port of Londonderry we were met by a steamtug, and passengers and mail for Ireland were taken off. Again we put to sea, and 180 miles further, including a sail up the Clyde, brought us to Glasgow. As soon as the ship reached the wharf, a revenue officer came aboard, followed by a man with a bucket of paste. The officer examined our baggage and finding it all right, the pasteman would stick on a card so that it could be taken ashore. The only articles looked for were liquor, tobacco, and American reprints of English copyrighted books. The latter article they regard as a kind of literary piracy which they will not tolerate, and if any such works are found they are committed to the flames.

At a proper time my turn came, and the officer with much politeness looked over my traps, but finding none

c

of these contraband articles in my valise it received a
card of approval, when I was allowed to go ashore.

ALONG THE CLYDE.

For thirty miles below Glasgow along the river Clyde,
there are fine cultivated farms presenting a beauty of
landscape scenery seldom met with in any other part of
the world. The land rises gradually from the river
back to the highlands, and this slope is covered with
fine farms and farm houses, including many beautiful
palaces occupied by Scottish nobility. Here can be
seen feeding on these green slopes the best breeds of
horses, cattle and sheep met with in any part of Europe.
And here, also, are seen sporting in these fields, the
large English rabbit, of various colors, from coal black,
to those of snowy whiteness.

Along the Clyde, there is almost one continuous village, with here and there a large town or city; all of
which are largely engaged in ship building. These
ships are all built of iron, and on every sea, and in every
port, the Clyde vessels are seen. On the right bank of
the river twenty miles below Glasgow, is the city of
Greenock, containing 50,000 inhabitants, and much
celebrated for its iron factories and ship yards. On the
opposite side of the river, eight miles above Greenock,
stands Dunbartin Castle, a place famous in Scottish
history. It was taken from the English by Wallace,
and its capture is regarded as the greatest exploit in the
career of that noted warrior. The castle is built on a

rock which stands out in the river, and is now occupied by a small garrison.

The river from this point is narrow, with shallow water, and can only be navigated by vessels of heavy tonage at high tide. Dredging machines are all the while employed deepening the channel, and the dirt is taken to fill up bayous, and make land along its banks.

GLASGOW.

Next to London, this is the largest city on the British Isles, and contains nearly half a million inhabitants. The city is well built, with wide streets, and contains many fine squares and parks. Its houses are mostly high, built of brown stone, and much blackened by coal smoke which gives to the city a dark and gloomy appearance. Glasgow is largely engaged in manufacturing iron ware, and ship building, and is the most commercial place in Scotland. It contains but few attractions for strangers. Although its history dates back to the sixth century, there is but one building of note which makes any claim to antiquity, and that is the Glasgow Cathedral. This is a fine, massive structure, and by the date on its walls shows that the first church on its site was dedicated in the sixth century.

On a high and beautiful knoll, east of the Cathedral, is located the old cemetery containing many monuments of distinguished men who lived in past ages; the highest and most conspicuous of which, is that of John Knox, the great reformer.

SOUTHERN SCOTLAND.

A person traveling through this country will be
surprised to find so much good land, and under so high
a state of cultivation, being equal to the best gardens
in the United States. Some idea of the product of a
farm may be formed, when we consider the average
rental of land is about nine dollars per acre. And with
these high rents, the tenant's lease, which in most cases
is perpetual, will sell for more than farms in Illinois.
But few farmers own the land which they occupy, as it
mostly belongs to noblemen whose ancestors obtained
it centuries ago through the old feudal rights. This
country is neither level nor hilly, but undulating and is
well adapted for farming purposes. All of the public
roads are narrow, not exceeding twenty feet, and are
macadamized with limestone. There is but little timber
in the country; more or less young trees are seen on
every farm, but they are more for ornament than use,
and the only native forest trees are seen in the parks of
noblemen. The fencing is composed of either stone
or hedge, the buildings are constructed mostly of
stone, and wooden buildings are not seen in this country.

Almost every part of southern Scotland is identified
with the history of past ages, and in traveling through
it a person will see many places where great events
have occurred. A short distance from Glasgow is
located the old Douglas Castle, a place famous in
Scottish history, now occupied by a descendant of
the great Douglases of former times, known as

Duke of Hamilton. Here is a large park of native forest trees, containing fountains, artificial lakes, and flower gardens. And in this park can be seen the different kinds of deer, as well as a large herd of native wild cattle, with their long black horns and shaggy hair. Close by this castle was fought the great battle of Bothwell Bridge.

Twenty-six miles west of Edinburgh we came to the old city of Falkirk, which is of great historical celebrity. One-half mile west of the town in the beautiful fields now covered with grain, is where Wallace fought his last battle, and by the treachery of one of his men was defeated, captured, carried to London, and executed on Tower Hill. On the east side of the city the place was, pointed out where Charles III. was defeated in the last battle fought by the Stuarts, for the crown of England.

Thirteen miles east of Falkirk, is still to be seen the Palace and Abbey of Linlithgrow, the birthplace of Queen Mary. These buildings stand on high ground by the side of a small lake, and are now in a state of ruins. The massive walls are still standing, which show them to have been fine specimens of architectural skill.

EDINBURGH.

The city of Edinburgh is very remarkable in its location, its limits extending over hill, valley and plain.

Adjoining it, on two sides are fine cultivated farms, while on the others rest Colton Hill, and Saulsbury crags; with the city of Leith extending to the bay, two

miles distant.   It has a population of 205,000, and contains many fine colleges and seminaries.   For the British
Isles it is considered the seat of learning, as well as the
cradle of fine arts.   The city consists of two parts—the
old and new town—divided by a deep valley. This
valley at one time contained an artificial lake, which
was used for sailing pleasure boats ; but a large part of
it is now used as a railroad station; the road passing
from it through tunnels under the city.   This plan of
railroads passing under a city instead of through it, is
very common in this country.   From the station the
street is reached by ascending long flights of stone
steps, and in places streets pass over this valley by
means of stone bridges, on which houses are built.

South of this valley lies the old town, built on a hillside, one street rising above another, giving to it a bold
and imposing appearance.   The houses are built with
brown stone, many of which are eight, and some ten
stories high.   At the upper end of the old town, and on
a high cliff of rocks three hundred and eighty feet above
the bay, overlooking the city and surrounding country,
stands Edinburgh Castle, a fortification famous in history.

There is but one entrance to this castle, which is across
a moat by a drawbridge.   At all other places it is guarded
by a high wall, built on cliffs of rocks, and is now
occupied by a regiment of soldiers.   In this castle is to
be seen the mammoth gun, called *Mons Meg*, famous in
history.   It is of great length, twenty-four inches in the
bore, and is made of thick bars of iron hooped together.
The inscription on its carriage, says it was made at

Brittainy, in the year 1476, and employed at the seige of Naham Castle in 1513. In 1682 it burst while firing a salute in honor of a visit from the Duke of York.

On the east side of the castle is the crown-room containing the insignia of Scottish royalty, among which is a crown, a sceptre, a sword of state, and the Lord Treasurer's rod of office, all of which are made of gold.

This regalia has been worn at the time of crowning every king of Scotland, from David I. to James VI.

On the ground floor of this wing of the castle, is Queen Mary's room, where the unfortunate Queen was kept while a prisoner in the castle, and in this room, she gave birth to James VI., in whom the crown of England and Scotland were united. On the east side of this room is the window from which the young prince was let down in a basket suspended by a rope, and was received by friends below, who conveyed him to Stirling Castle, where he was baptized in the Catholic faith. When this window was opened, I looked down from the giddy hight of two hundred and forty-two feet, and thought how few mothers there were, who would risk their infants but eight days old, in such a place.

From the castle we went down High street, our guide pointing out buildings on most every block, associated with Scottish history. Among other places were St. Giles church and the old parliment house. On this street is the Knox house, where lived and died the great reformer of whom Queen Mary once said: she feared his face more than all the armies of England. This house, according to the date on its walls, was built in

1490. The lower part of it is now used as a grocery, while the upper part is exhibited to the public, and contains the furniture of its former occupant. Fronting the door of the second story is a stone platform, surrounded by an iron railing, from which it is said, Knox frequently preached to the people in the street. Nearly opposite the Knox house is the Tweeddale Court, where once lived the Marquis of Tweeddale; and it was at the entrance of this mansion, that the misterious murder of Bigbie occurred.

At the east side of the city, and on flat land, which is almost on a level with the bay is situated the palace of Holyrood, the former residence of Scottish royalty. The grounds around this palace are very beautiful, being ornamented with shade trees and flower gardens, and enclosed by an iron fence twelve feet high. This palace is built of brown stone, very large, and contains an open court in the center, ninety feet square. The east wing is not open to visitors, being fitted up for royal guests, and is the home of Queen Victoria, when she visits Edinburgh. The picture gallery is the largest apartment in the palace, and on its walls are suspended the portraits of one hundred and six kings of Scotland, from Furgus I. who reigned (B. C. 330), to James VI.

Queen Mary's apartments are the most interesting of the palace, and remain the same as when last occupied by the unfortunate Queen. After passing through the audience room we entered the Queen's bedchamber, which contains her bed, as well as various articles of her furniture, all of which have an ancient appearance.

On one side of this room is the door through which the conspirators entered, and on the opposite side is the cabinet where they found their victim Riccio. Regardless of the tears and entreaties of the Queen, the unfortunate secretary was dragged into the audience room, and there dispatched with daggers. The exact spot where this occurred is pointed out by the keeper of these rooms, and he never forgets to show the visitors the stains of blood, still on the floor, where Riccio fell.

Adjoining the palace is the old Holyrood Abbey, built in 1128, but now in a state of ruin. The walls alone are still standing, and within its walls are the tombs of many of the kings of Scotland, as well as other distinguished men of past ages.

IRELAND.

Having sailed over one hundred miles, along the northern coast of Ireland, I had a fine view of the Giants Causeway, and Port Rush, which is the entrance to Londonderry, as well as many other places of interest. The scenery along this coast is very picturesque with clifts of rocks in many places rising perpendicularly from the waters edge, and back of which, are rocky, barren mountains, without a tree or shrub, and in some places without a single habitation. But it is very different in the interior of the country where the land is mostly level, and under a high state of cultivation. In some places are seen fine farm buildings surrounded by parks or fruit trees,

D

which belong to, and are occupied by wealthy Irish gentlemen. But the larger portion of the land belongs to noblemen who live in England, and who exact every farthing they can get from the poor tenants, leaving them scarcely enough to live on. If the tenant plants a tree he dare not cut it down, and if he keeps a dog he has to tie him up so the rabbits (which are claimed by the landlord) will not be molested. The fencing here consists of hedge, and the tenant houses are mostly mud hovels covered with thatch.

I visited the city of Belfast, which city is situated at the head of the bay, ten miles from the Irish sea, and is built on flat land which rises only a few feet above tide water. On the east side of the city are mountains which are without trees, or vegetation of any kind, while on the west side are fine, cultivated farms. Belfast contains 120,000 inhabitants, and is the greatest linen manufacturing city in the world. Linen Hall occupies a large square, and through it most of the wholesale linen trade is carried on. I went through one appartment of this hall, which is three hundred feet in length, and where linen thread was piled up on either side almost to the ceiling.

The railroad running south from Belfast, passes through a very rich country where there are many fine towns and cities. On this road we passed the battle field of Boyne, where James II. met William III., and on this field was decided, and sealed the fate of the Stuart family to the throne of England. A monument is here erected to commemorate that event.

Dublin, the Irish capital, contains a population of 250,000, and is well built, with wide streets, and high houses, many of which are coated with marble; and the general appearance of the city is pleasing and attractive. The city contains great wealth, and along its principal streets, are seen crowds of well dressed men and women, whose manners and personal appearance show a high state of refinement, unsurpassed by any other city in Europe. Probably there is no city on the British Isles, where the English language is so correctly spoken as here. The broad Irish brogue can scarcely be noticed among the better classes. Here in Dublin, as well as other cities of Ireland, the Irish jilting carts are in common use, and have almost taken the place of the cab.

The Prince of Wales, was on a visit to Dublin during the time I was there, and the streets, and public buildings were decorated with flags in honor of his visit. I saw the Prince pass through the street in an open car riage, drawn by six horses, with a groom riding each horse. Other carriages containing noblemen followed, and preceding the procession, was a company of dragoons, and all went on a gallop.

While I was in Dublin, George F. Train, of Fenian notoriety was arrested, and thrown in prison for a debt contracted some time before, on a purchase of railroad iron. One of Train's creditors who had just returned from holding a conference with him, said to me, that Train acknowledged that the claim, both principal

and interest, was just, but said it was contrary to his
principle, to pay interest, and contrary to his interest
to pay principal; consequently he could not liquidate
the debt without injuring both his conscience and
finances.

CHAPTER II.

ENGLAND.

After spending a few days in Dublin, we took passage for Liverpool, and had a pleasant sail across the Irish Sea. The steamer on which we were passengers had on board some three hundred Irish laborers, on their way to England. These people were poorly clad, and their baggage consisted of small packages tied up in bandana handkerchiefs, which they carried under their arms. Notwithstanding their poverty, I never met with a more jolly set of fellows, and their merry songs and witty jokes, kept the cabin passengers all the while in a roar of laughter. On the deck of the ship, they had an Irish dance, and having crowded on one side, caused the vessel to keel over so as to take in water. The officers tried in vain to disburse them, but the noise of the fiddle and bagpipe, together with the rattling of the feet of the dancers, drowned all other noise. At this crisis the captain threw from the hurricane deck a peice of old carpet down on the heads of the musicians, which broke

up the dance, and caused the crowd to separate. As we
sailed up the Mersey, we had a fine view of Liverpool with
its harbor and docks, presenting a forest of masts probably
unequalled in any other city in the world, excepting New
York. Liverpool has a black, smoky appearance, being
a great manufacturing, as well as a commercial city; but
contains very few attractions for a stranger. After remaining one day here, we took the cars for London, two
hundred and two miles distant. The country between
these points, is very fine, being a continuation of well
cultivated farms, with fine stone farm houses, and hedge
fences. There is no timber here except ornamental trees
and parks belonging to noblemen; and the land is level,
highly cultivated, and so densely populated, that it
appears like one continuous village.

A person from the United States, in traveling through
this country, will be surprised at its smallness, in
comparison to our own as a few hours only are
required by railroad to travel across it from sea, to sea.
A Yankee, on visiting England, said the island was so
small that he was afraid to turn around, as he would be
in danger of stepping off into the ocean.

LONDON.

The city of London is located mostly on the north
side of the Thames, and is twelve miles in length, by
nine in breadth, and contains over three million inhabitants, being about one-fifth of the whole population of
England. The old town, or city proper is but a small

portion of London, although most of the business is done there. The streets in this part of the city are mostly narrow and crooked, many of which are merely alleys, not wide enough for two carriages to pass each other. There are a few streets of reasonable width which are the great thoroughfares of the city, and during business hours show as much activity as Broadway New York. Most of the houses are built of brick, and have a black dirty appearance. The white stone fronts, look as though they were coated with tar, caused by the burning of soft coal. London was at one time a walled city, and two of its gates are still standing, with a small portion of its wall. But from being a city hemmed in by walls, it has expanded in all directions, forming connection with other places, and absorbing towns and villages for miles around.

There are no street cars here, the width of the streets not admitting them, but there are underground railroads running in tunnels under the city, which have stations at the principal streets. The trains stop at each station about one half minute, then go off again at a fearful rate, causing the buildings over the road to tremble and shake, on the passage of each train. These roads have upper stations above ground, which are reached by long flights of stone steps, and the roads and cars are well lighted. Crowds of people can be seen hurrying hither and thither, by means of these roads, the same as though they were above ground.

The public buildings of London are mostly constructed of white stone, but have a black, smoky appearance. St.

Paul's Church is the most prominent object in the great metropolis. It stands on Ludgate Hill, near the center of the city, and its lofty dome rises high above the surrounding buildings which can be seen for miles away. It is built in the form of a cross, five hundred and fourteen feet long by two hundred and eighty-six feet wide, and surmounted with two towers and a dome, the latter is three hundred and seventy-five feet high. Painted on the inside of the dome, are six large pictures, illustrating scenes in the life of St. Paul. Westminster Palace, or House of Parliament, stands on the bank of the Thames in the west division of the city. This palace has frequently been spoken of as exceeding in size and beauty of design all other palaces in England. It is very showy on the outside, but the inside looks more like a prison than a palace; being badly lighted and ventilated. The house of Lords as well as that of Commons is small, not being capable of seating all the members when there is a full attendance. The walls and ceilings of these halls are partly covered with gilt, which gives them a glaring appearance that is unpleasant to the eye, and the seats consist of benches covered with red morocco, and running lengthwise like an old fashioned school house. There are no tables in front of the seats for writing, nor pages to attend the members, and they have but few of the conveniences seen in the legislative halls at Washington.

Fronting the House of Parliament is located Westminster Abbey, which has been so often referred to by English historians. Its history dates back almost to the time of the first introduction of Christianity into England. Here, William the Conqueror was crowned, as well as many other English sovereigns. The Abbey including its chapels and halls, covers eight acres of ground, and here can be seen the tombs of many of the ancient kings and queens of England, with that of Queen Elizabeth by the side of her rival, Mary Queen of Scotland. In one part of the Abbey called the poets corner, I saw the tombs of Milton, Campbell, Sheriden, Shelly, and many other distinguished poets.

The bank of England is located a few squares from London Bridge, and covers an area of several acres, including a whole square. In the center of this building there is an open square where trees and grass are growing, and a fountain of water playing. The bank employs over one thousand clerks, has a steam press to print its own bills, and is without doubt the greatest money institution in the world.

On Cheapsides, one of the principal streets of the city, there is a curious clock which attracts much attention. This clock is very large, hanging over the sidewalk, and above it are the life size figures of three men and a woman; and by the side of each are bells of various sizes so as to chime. At the time of striking one of the figures representing a Scottish chief strikes his bell with a hammer when the others join by striking their bells making fine music, after which the chief strikes the hour. Large crowds of people collect here at the time of striking, and for this cause the authorities threaten to take it down.

E

One day as I was crowding my way through the street near London Bridge, first turning to the right, then to the left, then being run against by different ones, and my corns tramped on, I met a man with such a singular appearance, that I turned back to follow him in order to learn something of his business. He wore across his shoulder, a wide leather belt, on which appeared in large brass letters, "Rat catcher," and there were on the belt, cut in brass, many life size figures of rats. This rat catcher had a dog with him, to assist in his business, and said to me, that he caught rats alive, and sold them to sporting gentlemen for two pence apiece.

At different times I visited the Spurgeon Tabernacle to hear the great orator. This church is very large, with two tiers of galleries extending all the way around it, and will seat over six thousand people. Notwithstanding its great size, it is always filled at time of service, and hundreds of people are turned away who cannot get seats. Mr. Spurgeon is a stout heavy set man, with a broad face, and a strong clear voice, but I could see nothing in his preaching, to cause the world to run crazy after him.

Along Cheapsides and Old Broad Street I observed signs on business houses, which date their origin back a hundred or more years, as the time of establishing the firm; which firms have been handed down from father to son ever since—unlike our own country, where a man will make and lose a fortune, or change his business every few years. I read on one of these signs: "James Ray, Cutlery, established in 1572." Out of curiosity

I went into the store, where a clerk took me back to the counting room and introduced me to Mr. Ray, the proprietor, who was a young looking man, with pleasing address. He gave me a seat and we entered into conversation; when I remarked that his house, judging from its sign, was an old one, "Yes," said he, "I have been in this business for nearly three hundred years." I replied, you must have been young when you commenced business, Said he; "Yes rather," laughing, "when I speak of the firm I always include my ancestors." On the 25th of June, 1572, James Ray commenced business on this corner, and it has been continued by his posterity ever since without changing the name of the firm. He conducted me into a back room and pointed to the original sign of the firm which was painted nearly three hundred years ago.

THE TOWER OF LONDON.

This old fortification stands on the bank of the Thames, below London Bridge, and has been spoken of in history as a fort, a prison, a palace, a chapel, and a court of justice. It covers thirteen acres of ground, and is surrounded by a high wall, on the outside of which is a moat one hundred and twenty feet wide. This moat can be flooded with water from the river at high tide, and is crossed at the main entrance to the tower by a draw bridge. After passing through the inner wall, we came to the traitor's gate, where state criminals were brought into the tower by water. Within the walls are thirteen towers, the largest of which is White Tower, ninety-two feet high, with walls fifteen feet thick, and was built by William the Conqueror, in the year 1070. In this tower is St. John's Chapel, where the ancient kings attended worship, and in which many of them were crowned. Over the chapel is a dark, ill-ventilated room, where Sir Walter Raleigh was confined twelve years preceding his execution. This room was also the prison of William Wallace, Lord Hastings, and Lady Jane Gray.

From White Tower we went into a large hall, containing thirty life size figures, clad in armor, and mounted on horses, representing kings, warriors, and noblemen of past ages. Here are also many figures on foot, covered with armor, made of polished steel, covering the wearer all over, and proof against spear, or sword. This armor is the same worn by the person here represented, and by which we can see the size and form of the former kings and warriors of England, from Edward II. to James I., all of whom are holding in their hand the same sword used by them in time of war. We were shown the block and axe, used in beheading Anne Boleyn, Earl of Essex, and many other state criminals. We next came to the Jewel Tower, containing. the jewels of state, among which are St. Edward's crown, which was used at all the coronations from Charles I., to William IV.; and here is also the new crown made for the coronation of Queen Victoria, valued at a half million dollars. There is to be seen the Queen's Diadem, the Royal Scepter, St. Edward's Staff, and Sword of Justice and Mercy, Coronation Bracelets, and Royal

Spurs, with many other articles, all made of massive gold, ornamented with diamonds.

Near the center of the Tower grounds is a small green spot surrounded by an iron railing, the place for private executions. Tower Hill, where state criminals were publicly executed, is a slight eminence outside of the Tower walls, and is surrounded by a high iron fence. The ground is now covered with flowers, and ornamental trees, and no longer a place of execution.

There are 1500 soldiers of the royal guard, quartered in the Tower, and also many conductors, (called beef eaters), whose business it is to conduct visitors through the Tower, and explain to them, things of interest. Visitors pay one shilling each, for a ticket of admission, and are under the guardianship of these conductors, and if they stray away from them they are liable to be arrested and placed in the guard house.

CHAPTER III.

After a stay of twelve days in London, we left for the Continent, by the way of New Haven and Dieppe. The country through which we passed is not so good as the north or central parts of England. Here the soil is light and underlaid with chalk beds. In some places the embankments of the railroads are composed of pure chalk, giving to them a white, shining appearance. At New Haven, we went aboard of a steamer bound for Dieppe, France, a distance of sixty-four miles. The coast of France, as seen from sea, has a beautiful appearance, with its chalky bluffs rising perpendicularly above the water, looking like walls of marble. Behind these bluffs are seen forest trees, and farm houses; the coast differing very much from that of England and Ireland, where scarcely a tree or a shrub can be seen along its borders.

Dieppe is an old seaport city, largely engaged in the fish and lumber trade, and its harbor consists of a walled basin which is connected with the sea by a narrow channel guarded by strong fortifications. The city is built of white stone, and from the sea, it presents a bold and imposing appearance. Here for the first time, we saw the French fisher women, so often referred to by travelers, and it was amusing to see a large collection of these women gathered around a vessel, with their large fish baskets, waiting their turn to have them filled. Their short dresses, loose, dirty, jackets, and white caps gave them a comical appearance. Dieppe has figured extensively in the history of France, and has been the scene of many hard fought battles. It was here the French, under the leadership of the Maid of Orleans, Joan of Arc, defeated the British, and drove them from the country; and in return the British fleet attacted, subdued, and burned the city.

The country from Dieppe to Paris, a distance of one hundred and fifty miles, is very fine, showing a rich soil, and under a high state of cultivation. There is no fencing in this country, except that inclosing railroads; and stock is guarded while feeding on the pasture, by a herdsman, or more frequently by a woman and a dog. The land in this country generally belongs to the occupant, and the boundaries of each farm, are shown by the different kinds of grain.

Seventy-two miles from Dieppe, we came to the old city of Rouen, formerly the capital of Normandy, and the place where William the Conquorer fitted out his expedition for the conquest of England. This city is built on both sides of the river Seine, and contains many fine public buildings, some of which have an ancient appearance. After a stay of three hours in Rouen, we again took the train for Paris, and found quarters at the Grand Hotel de Orleans.

PARIS.

A person visiting Paris, cannot fail to notice the great difference between it and London. Although only two hundred and eighty miles apart, they differ in almost every particular, not only in the general appearance of the cities, but in language, customs, and habits of the people. London is mostly built of brick; having narrow, crooked streets. The buildings are blacked with smoke, and business appears to be the main object of its citizens. While Paris is built of white stone, the streets are mostly wide, clean, and attractive in appearance, and the enjoyment of life, and pleasure are the grand objects of the people. No factories, using steam power, are to be seen in the fashonable parts of Paris, and iron works with forging hammers are not allowed within its walls. Everything appears to have been done to make it attractive; and partly from this cause, it now has nearly two million of inhabitants, and is the great metropolis of the continent, as well as the largest, and most wealthy city in the world—London only excepted.

Paris is surrounded by a stone wall, fifteen miles in length, thirty feet high, and eleven feet thick, with a ditch on the outside, forty feet wide. On this wall are ninety-four batteries, or forts, consisting of ramparts and parapets mounted with heavy cannon. Through this wall are seventy-one gates, where toll is collected for the benefit of the city. On the inside of the wall there is a railroad running nearly the whole way around the city.

The river Seine runs through the central part of the city; its banks are walled up to the level of the streets, and crossed by many stone bridges. Small steamboats run up and down the river carrying passengers to the different parts of the city, as well as towns and cities in the vicinity of Paris. There is but little commerce on the river; and its banks unincumbered by docks and warehouses, are used for driveways and pleasure grounds. There are many boulevards running in various directions through the city, which constitute its principal thoroughfares. These boulevards are about three times the width of common streets—shaded with trees, and paved with composition; which makes them almost as smooth as a marble floor. New boulevards are being made through different parts of the city, by pulling down fine blocks of buildings, and converting the ground they occupy into public use.

On the bank of the Seine, near the center of the city, is located the Louvre containing the great French museum. This is the largest building in Paris, and perhaps the largest in the world. This building consists of a number of royal palaces built by different kings of France, all joined together, and forming three sides of a large public square, the Tuileries forming the fourth side. The square on the inside of the Louvre consists

F

in several acres of ground, through which is a driveway
passing through an arch under the building, and in the
middle of the square is a small flower garden, with
ornamental trees, and a fountain of water.

Adjoining the garden of the Tuileries, is the square
of Concorde, containing many fountains, and groups of
collossal statues, some of which, represent different cities
of France. In the center of this square, stands the great
Egyptian obelisk, eighty feet high, which was brought
from the valley of the Nile, in the year 1836. On this
square, Louis XVI. was beheaded, and many other scenes
memorable in French history took place.

On the west of the square Concorde is the Champs
Elysess, a great avenue one mile in length, and a quarter
of a mile in width, containing beautiful parks with
flower gardens, where birds are singing, bands of music
playing, and fountains of water sparkling in the sunbeams, making it the most attractive place in Paris.
On this avenue are seen almost every afternoon, driving
back and fourth, the Emperor and suit, as well as the
nobility and fashionable people of Paris. But excelling
all others in point of extravagance is the gazells, with
their fine carriages and servants in livery; some times
accompanied by a Duke or Count. These women have
great wealth, but no virtue. They exercise great
influence in the city, dictating the fashions for Paris
and the world.

At the Hippodrome there is a baloon ascension almost
every afternoon; a rope being attached to the baloon, by
this means it is brought down again by steam power.

In this baloon, I made an aerial voyage to see the city, and was much delighted with the scenery, exceeding in beauty and grandeur, anything that I had ever seen. When the baloon was loosed from its fastening, it went up with great rapidity, for a few hundred feet, after which the ascent was more gradual until it reached its highest point. And here the view was grand beyond description ; the whole city and surrounding country, for many miles were visible, looking like a painted panorama. The different currents of air caused the baloon to float back and forth, sometimes over one street, then over another, while the moving mass of people, horses and carriages below, appeared about the size of children's toys. As we again approached *terra firma* the mammoth baloon began to pitch around like a kite in a high storm, making it almost impossible for a person to stand up in the basket. At last the baloon came within reach of the grappling hooks, and was brought to anchor.

In the South part of the city, is located the foundling asylum, where all the waifs of the city are received, and no questions asked. From the street there is an open court, the entrance into the asylum, and on one side of which is a raised platform containing a basket. Into this basket the child is placed, and the bell rung, when up it goes through the dark passage, and is cared for, above.

Under the city are many large sewers, or canals used for the supply, and waste of water. Some of these canals are miles in length, and are kept in repair by people who live in them. Gas is kept burning at all times to keep these passages lighted, and a railroad track is laid along them, on which people travel from place to place in hand cars. There are also small rowboats capable of carrying four persons, each running on these underground canals, and in these, people pass to and fro, the same as above ground. I took a short ride on these subterranean thoroughfares, but found underground canals and railroads was not the most pleasant way of traveling.

The catacombs of Paris are situated in the south part of the city, and cover a large space of ground, which originally was a stone quarry, where stone was obtained for building the city. It is now converted into a vast bone receptical, whither have been conveyed millions of the dead. the products of exhumations made in the ancient cemeteries of Paris

A short distance from the Tuileries is the great stock exchange (called the Bourse), where all the business is transacted, by thirty men, who are authorized by government, to do brokerage business, and no transaction is legal unless endorsed by these men. On the first floor of this building there is a large hall, in the center of which is a bar where the brokers are seated; and parties wishing to buy or sell stock, are admitted to this hall by paying a tribute to the government. Spectators are allowed to go on the floor above and look down on the crowded, and excited mass below. At two o'clock each day, the sales commence, and I never saw anything to equal the excitement of the traders. Some rising on tiptoes, with both arms extended, their eyes glaring

like a mad man's, with sweat running down their faces
in large drops, as they sing out at the top of their voice:
"One more centime on the last bid." Excitement in
business transactions is peculiar to Frenchmen. A Wall
street broker can buy and sell stocks all day, make a
fortune and loose it again, besides cheating his neighbor
broker out of all he is worth, without changing a muscle
of his face.

The gayest places in Paris are the wine gardens,
where they have public balls every night. These are
attended by thousands of people of all classes. Bal
Mabille and Luxembourg gardens are the principal ones
where the gay and fashionable people of both sexes
collect for amusements. These places consist of a large
dancing hall opening into a park, where fountains of
water are playing, and flowers blooming beside the beautiful walks and avenues. In the middle of the dance
room is a platform seating twenty-four musicians, and a
thousand or more persons can dance at a time. When
ordinary tunes are played, the dancing is the same as at
other balls, but when the band play a particular air the
dancing exceeds all description—the men throwing their
feet in all directions with, their bodies in all sorts of
positions. The girls with loud laughs and merry jokes,
in order to excell their partners, do many strange things
which are tolerated no where else but in the public balls
of Paris.

CHAPTER IV.

BELGIUM.

After a stay of twenty days in Paris, we took the cars for the north, and for two hundred miles we traveled through French territory. The country on this route is very fine, having the appearance of the prairies of the west, with large undulating plains, without fencing, or farm houses, while here and there, can be seen a grove of timber. The land is rich, under a high state of cultivation, and the farmers mostly live in villages. At a small town on the Belgian frontier, all the baggage belonging to travelers was taken into the custom house, where it underwent examination. And a few miles further, we came to the famous old city of Mons, which is built on flat land, on both sides of the river Trouille, and surrounded by an earth fortification.

Belgium is a level country, and portions of the north part of it, along the coast, are very flat, being on a level with the sea, where dikes are built to prevent the lands from being overflowed at high tide. All kinds of grain common to the United States, except corn, are raised here. Flax, hemp, chiccory, and madder, are extensively cultivated. Wild poppies grow in this country, and, when in bloom the fields look like a vast flower garden. They are the same annoyance to the people here as the Canada thistles are to the New England farmers. Many of the public roads are paved with stone, like the streets of a city, and are shaded on either side by trees, which add much to the beauty of the country. There are many artificial groves in this country, most of which belong to the government. The forest of Soignies, near Brussels, is ten miles long and five miles wide consisting of beech trees, standing in rows about ten feet apart, are tall and straight, being sixty or eighty feet without limbs. This forest was planted seventy-eight years ago, and is considered the finest in Europe.

The old fashioned windmills of former ages are still in use here, and continue to grind the grain of the country. These mills are built of stone, very high and tapering like a tower, and on the top of which is a large wind-wheel to move the machine. It is said some of these mills have been standing for more than one thousand years.

Dogs are made useful here being bought and sold like horses or cattle, and when hitched to a truck wagon or a wheel-barrow it is surprising to see what a load they will draw. One day I saw a man peddling vegetables with a small wagon drawn by a woman and a dog. The woman was leaning forward with the harness across her breast, and the dog with his tongue out was also pulling his best, while the man walked beside the wagon smoking his pipe.

There are many different languages spoken in Belgium; each section of country having its own dialect; French, Flemish, Dutch, and German, are more or less spoken.

BRUSSELS.

The capital of Belgium contains a population of 237,000 and is regarded a model city, possessing much of the beauty and attraction of Paris without its noise and confusion. The city consists of two parts, the old and the new, differing very much from each other. In the new part, the streets are wide, the buildings are constructed of white stone and have a clean, attractive appearance. There is a boulevard running part way around the city between the old and new town which is six miles long, three hundred feet wide and has three driveways, shaded by seven rows of trees. The grand park occuping a central part of the city is said to be the most beautiful one in Europe, containing large elm trees which were planted one hundred and twenty years ago. Here is a dense forest where birds are singing, squirrels chattering, and were it not for the fine marble statuary, and fountains of water playing, a person might imagine himself in an American forest, instead of being in the midst of a populous city.

The old Brussels Cathedral is located near the

center of the city being built in the twelfth century and
contains many fine paintings and statuary. But the
most remarkable item of its contents is the pulpit,
which is carved in oak, and represents the expulsion of
Adam and Eve from Paradise. These figures are all
life size, and the offenders are being driven forth from
the Garden of Eden by an Angel, with a flaming
sword. Behind these figures stands Death with a dart
in his hand, and by the side of which is the tree of
knowledge supporting a globe. The canopy over the
pulpit is supported by two angels, on the top of which
is the Virgin Mary, holding the infant Savior.

Close to the Cathedral, is the old Royal Palace, now
used as a town hall. This is a fine old gothic structure
with a tower three hundred and sixty-four feet high,
on the top of which stands a gilt statue of St. Michael.
It was in the grand hall of this palace that Charles V.
held his courts, and in it, he signed his abdication of
the throne in favor of his son Phillip.

No city in the world can compete with Brussels in the
manufacture of lace, and from this source it has derived
much of its wealth. I visited some of these lace factories, and saw the operatives, (who were all women),
weaving it. All fine lace is woven by hand, as a
genuine article cannot be made in any other way.

The present King of Belgium, Leopold II. is a young
looking man, of very common appearance; and the
Queen is a sister of the late Emperor Maximillian of
Mexico. She drives out almost every afternoon in a
carriage drawn by four ponies, holding the reins in

G

her own hands, and using the whip freely. Two
grooms ride behind the carriage to render assistance if
necessary.

WATERLOO.

Eleven miles south-east of Brussels, we came to the
village of Waterloo, which is composed of a large
collection of farm houses, and looks as though it might
have been built soon after the deluge. Here is a church
which was built three hundred years ago, and around
it are monuments to the memory of a number of English
officers who fell at Waterloo. Close by the church is
the house where the Marquis of Anglesea's leg was
amputated, and the owner of this house finds it a profit-
able business, exhibiting the boot, belonging to the
amputated leg. The leg of the Marquis was buried in
the church yard, and over it stands a monument erected
to its memory.

Two miles from here is the battle field of Waterloo,
near the center of which, stands the great monument,
built by the King of Holland, on the spot where his
son the Prince of Orange was wounded. This monument
is built of dirt, two hundred feet high, and covering
four acres of ground, looking at a distance like an
Egyptian Pyramid. Four hundred Belgian women
were engaged two years in its construction, carrying
dirt in baskets placed on their heads. On the top of
this monument stands a colossal lion, cast from cannon
taken at the battle. The head of this lion is turned

towards France, his tail erect, a ball under one fore foot and his mouth open as if in the act of growling.

The land where this battle was fought, consists of fine, cultivated farms, and is nearly level, with a slight depression running across the middle of it, which was the dividing line between the contending armies. Our guide, who is an old Belgian soldier, and fought in the battle says: fifty-three years have made but little change in this place. The ground is now covered with grain the same as it was on that eventful day. The same farm buildings are still standing, and show marks of cannon balls. In the south part of the field is the Chateau of Hougomont, which was considered the key of the position, and withstood the many assaults from the French army. The high wall around the garden as well as the little chapel, dwelling, barn, and out-buildings, are all constructed of brick, and still show the marks of the dreadful conflict.

ANTWERP.

This great commercial metropolis of Belgium, stands on the south-east side of the river Scheldt, and contains over 100,000 inhabitants. The river at this point, is both wide and deep, forming one of the finest harbors in the German Ocean. Antwerp is an old city, and has figured extensively in the early history of Europe, and was the capital of Flanders, when the Spaniards were in possession of it. Its streets are narrow and crooked, winding and turning in all directions, so that a stranger

has great difficulty in finding his way through them.
Many of the houses are six or seven stories high, and
tapering up to a pinnacle, with their fronts adorned
with tracery work, and have heavy bars of iron across
the windows, to guard the inmates against the assault of
the enemy in time of war. A stroll through the streets
of Antwerp is very amusing, as we see the peculiar
costume of the market women, with their large straw
hats, loose jackets, and wooden shoes, which appear in
harmony with the old buildings around them. While
the gay toilets of the girls, consisting of a great variety
of colors, with their white lace caps, and green jackets
are in keeping with the picturesque appearance of the
city.

The great cathedral of Notre Dame, which was built
in the thirteenth century, is a magnificent structure being
five hundred feet in length, two hundred and fifty in
breadth, and contains many beautiful paintings and
statuary. Its spire is the most remarkable part of the
structure, and attracts universal admiration, towering
up four hundred and six feet in hight, and is considered
the most beautiful shaft in the world.

Vandyke and Rubens, whose paintings adorn the
walls of all the principal galleries of Europe, lived and
died at Antwerp, and here their monuments are to be
seen.

There are many curious customs in Antwerp, although
not confined exclusively to this city, but are seen here
to the greatest extent. Large crowds of men and women
are seen in the principal beer saloons, drinking and

smoking in full enjoyment of life. This habit is not confined to the low and profligate, but the well dressed respectable gentleman and lady, are seen here, even at the late hour of night. Wooden shoes cut out of a block of wood, are worn here by the poor people. Rolls of bread the size of a man's arm, and five or six feet in length, are in common use. I have frequently seen people carrying on their shoulder a large bundle of these rolls. At restaurants these rolls are set up against the wall, and cut off from, as occasion requires.

The Zoological gardens of Antwerp are among the finest in Europe, and in them, animals are raised to supply menageries, and gardens of other countries. While in these gardens, I saw people engaged in conveying a tiger to a steamer, for shipment to England. In moving the tiger through the streets of the city, it became enraged, broke out of its cage, attacked and killed a man instantly. It was followed and dispatched with guns.

HOLLAND.

Holland is certainly a remarkable country, being (with a few exceptions) without a hill or knoll, or a stream of running water, and with a large portion of its surface lying below the level of the ocean. In many places along the beach, dykes are built to prevent the water of the sea from overflowing the country. These dykes were built and are kept in repair at the cost of millions of dollars which is raised by a tax levied on land in each district, guarded by them. At one time according to history, this country was a vast marsh uninhabited, and was swept over by the tide of the ocean; and it is to the industry and enterprise of its people that they owe, not only their wealth, and high commercial position, but even the land they occupy.

The draining of the land is done by means of canals which run everywhere through the country, connecting with each other, and forming a complete network. On each farm are sluice-ways, twelve or fourteen feet wide, and a few rods apart, at the terminus of which is a windmill, to pump the water up into the small canals. From these small canals, the water is pumped up still higher into the large ones, which empty into the sea. Each farmer pays a large amount of money, yearly, to the government, for the privilege of pumping the water off his lands. The water courses through the farms, answers in place of fencing, and the small canals are used for conveyance of produce from place to place, while through the main ones, the commerce of the country is carried on. These main canals are elevated high above the common level of the country, and mostly shaded on either side, by ornamental trees, while roads cross them on turn bridges. Steamboats, sloops, as well as other crafts, run on them, constituting the principal highways of Holland.

While traveling on one of these main canals, we had a fine view of the country. From the hurricane deck of the steamer, we could see large herds of cattle, sheep and goats, feeding on the rich meadows below us. The farmers were busily engaged with their hay crop, loading it into boats, instead of wagons, to convey it to their barns. The small canals running through the farms occupy the place of roads, and on them, people travel from place to place. If a farmer goes to church or visiting, he takes a boat, and if a young man goes courting, he does the same.

The mills for pumping water are the most conspicuous feature of the country; the high towers constructed of brick, tapering towards the top, with a mammoth wind-wheel on their top, can be seen at a great distance. During the wet season of the year, the pumps are kept running day and night, to prevent the country from being inundated.

Holland is without timber, except brush and ornamental trees. Much of the timber used here, comes from Switzerland, and the coal from England. Wheat, barley, and rye, are raised here to some extent, but grass is the principal crop, and beef, butter, and cheese, constitute the principal exports.

We traveled from Antwerp, to Rotterdam, by steamboat. The distance between these points by the way of the North Sea, is over two hundred miles. But a canal of ten miles in length, has been cut across the country connecting the waters, so that the distance by this route is only sixty miles. The country along this route is about equally divided between land and water. Many places, dykes are built along the shore, rising some feet above tide water, and hiding the view of the land, even from the hurricane deck of the steamer. The lofty towers of windmills, and spires of churches and school houses, with which the country abounds, appear to rise as it were out of the sea, while the buildings to which they belong, were not visible from the hurricane deck of the steamer.

On our passage, we saw a large number of sea lions basking on the sandbars at low tide. Some of these were as large as an ox, being ten or twelve feet in length, of various colors, and at a distance, they looked like herds of cattle.

I visited all the principal cities of Holland, and a short account of some of these is given below.

ROTTERDAM.

This is a large commercial city, being the second in Holland, in point of population, and the first for its maritime importance. It is situated on the north bank of the river Maas, which here resembles an arm of the sea although twenty miles from its mouth. Rotterdam has a population of over 100,000, and has a large inland, as well as foreign commerce. It is principally built of brick, which are small in size, and of a dark color differing from the brick of other countries. The houses are from four to six stories high; many of which are wider at the top than at the bottom, which gives to them a leaning appearance, and look as though they were about to fall into the street. At many of the windows are looking-glasses suspended from the wall on the outside, so that the inmates of each room can see the people pass and repass, on the sidewalk. On one house I counted twenty-seven glasses, being three at each window. These looking-glasses at the windows are more or less used in all the cities of Holland.

Rotterdam is built on flat land, which rises only a few feet above tide water, and has many canals running through it, most of which are shaded with trees. Many of these canals are wide enough for large ships to turn in them, and the streets cross these canals by draw-bridges.

HAGUE.

The capital of Holland is situated three miles from the North Sea, and contains a population of 76,000. It has but little commerce, or manufacturing, but is a place of great beauty, and contains much of the wealth, as well as the aristocracy, and nobility of Holland. The city stands on flat land, containing many beautiful parks, flower gardens and artificial lakes, as well as numerous canals, with their banks shaded by ornamental trees.

Three miles from Hague, on the beach of the North Sea, is situated the old town of Scheveningen, made famous by poets, and writers of romance. It has no harbor, and is only accessible to fishing crafts, but it is the great bathing place for Holland. A large hotel is built here with a beer garden, extending down to the edge of the water, and here people collect to drink and smoke, while listening to the bands of music. Among those who appeared to enjoy themselves on the evening

H

of my visit here, were the King, two princes, and Prince
of Orange.   The present King of Holland, William III.
is a large fleshy Dutchman, and looks as though he were
a better judge of a good dinner, or a bottle of porter,
than the practical affairs of the kingdom.

AMSTERDAM.

According to history, Amsterdam was at one time the
greatest commercial city in the world.   Then its sails
were on every sea, while its ships were seen in every
port.   It has lost much of its trade, but still is a city of
great commercial importance, and contains 270,000
inhabitants.   Amsterdam is frequently styled the Venice
of the North, on account of its numerous canals, and its
similarity of situation to the Queen of the Adriatic.
The streets are mostly narrow and crooked, turning and
winding about in all directions, making it difficult for a
stranger to find his way.   The houses are high, many
of them running up to a sharp peak in the center, and
built out of range, showing no system in their construction.   And many of the houses are built leaning towards
the middle of the street so as to give additional room
above, forming almost an archway where the sun seldom
penetrates.   Almost every other street has a canal in
the middle of it, which gives water communication to
all parts of the city.

While in Amsterdam, we stopped at the Old Bible
Hotel, which has been so often referred to, by church
historians, as being the building where the Bible was

first printed, for the use of the public, when the Pope issued his bull against it, consigning all concerned in its publication, to the bottomless pit. A copy of the first edition of the Bible is here, for the inspection of the guests of the hotel, which bears date A. D. 1542. This building has been used for a hotel one hundred and twenty-two years, and is a great place of resort for English, and American travelers. A large gilt Bible hangs over the front door, opened at the first chapter of Matthew, and exhibiting four pictures of scriptural scenes. This sign has hung here ever since the house was opened as a hotel, and without close inspection, a person would think it a genuine Bible, instead of a painted sign.

The city of Amsterdam is situated on the Amstel Sea which is only navigable for ships of light tonage. All large vessels are obliged to pass through the North Holland canal, which is fifty miles in length. A new canal is now being constructed across the isthmus of North Holland, which will shorten the distance out to sea.

We left Amsterdam in a steamship, bound for Hamburg, which is about three hundred miles distant, and for about twenty hours, we encountered a heavy sea. Some twenty miles from shore, we passed an English steamer, beached on a sandbar, with the waves breaking over her, being a total wreck. Seventy miles sail up the river Elbe, brought us to the great commercial city of Hamburg.

CHAPTER V.

HAMBURG.

This is the most commercial city in the north of Europe, and ships from all parts of the world, are seen in its harbor. The flag of the Chinese junk, and the stars and stripes are seen waving beside the union jack of English merchantmen. Ten ocean steamships, run between here and New York, and most of the emigrants from northern Europe, take shipping here. The city has a population of near 200,000, and is said to contain more wealth, than any other city in Germany. In the old part of the city next to the river, the streets are narrow and crooked, but the new part is well built with wide streets high stone houses, which are of the modern there style of architecture. In the north part of the city is a beautiful lake, of some miles in circumference, called Alster's Basin. Fourteen little steamers run on it, to carry passengers to different points. This lake is walled up to the level of the street, and has a fine driveway around it, which is shaded with trees, and here is the great promenade of the city.

Hamburg, is one of the four independent cities of Germany, made so by the Confederation of the Rhine, and makes its own laws, same as other German States. Outside of the city limits, the territory belongs to Prussia, and on the opposite side of the river, are the borders of the late kingdom of Hanover.

Fifty-six miles from Hamburg brought us to the fine old city of Lubeck.

HANOVER.

Having parted with my company at Hamburg, I crossed the Elbe, and made a short tour through the old kingdom of Hanover. Much of the country is very fine, with highly cultivated farms, being equal in point of fertility, to any that I have seen in Europe. But towards the government I found a bitter feeling, as the annexation of that country to Prussia, makes all men eligible soldiers, besides oppressing them with a heavy taxation.

While traveling in this country, I met with an adventure, and on account of its oddity I will relate: Leaving the railroad line, I took the stage-coach to go some miles in the country, to see a curious old castle, which I had heard much about. On arriving at my destination, I inquired at the village inn, for a guide, but found no one who could speak English, or give any answer to my inquries. News went through the village that an American was at the hotel, and in a few minutes the bar-room was full of people, all anxious to see the sight.

If the landlord had been a Yankee, he would have charged admittance fees at the door, which would have amounted to a nice little sum. The crowd continued to increase, and I found myself an object of notoriety which was everything else but agreeable. At last an old man was brought, one who had been a sailor in his younger days, and knew a little English. I employed him to show me the castle, and we left the hotel followed by a large company of boys, as though I was a wild animal on exhibition.

On our return to the hotel, I found a message from a lady, requesting me to call on her. I was much surprised to find that I had been getting up a sensation, and after brushing up a little, I told my guide to take me to the lady's residence. On arriving at her house, I was introduced to an old lady, so big and fat, that she could hardly rise without help, from an arm-chair, where she was sitting. She explained through the interpreter her object in sending for me, by saying, that she had never seen an American, and was anxious to see how they looked. Then added, "I see you look like other folks, except a little taller." She continued, "I thought Americans were red." I explained to her, that Indians, the native Americans, were red. She then asked me if I was not an Indian, to which I replied, my ancestors were from Europe, and no way connected with the Indian race. She continued, "Do people out there dress as you do?" I replied, much the same. "Law me I thought they wore buckskin, and wrapped themselves up in buffalo robes," she responded.

She next inquired of me if I knew in America, Hans Schmidt, (John Smith in English). I replied, that I knew him well. At this news, she appeared much delighted, as she had heard nothing from him since he left Hanover, twenty-five years ago. But I told her the one I knew, was a different man, although of the same name. It never had occurred to her, that there was more than one John Smith living in America.

LUBECK.

The city of Lubeck, is situated at the south end of the Baltic Sea, and like Hamburg, is one of the four independent cities of Germany, and contains a population of 52,000. The streets of Lubeck, are like most other old cities of Germany, narrow and crooked, and the houses with their red tile roofs, running up to a pinnacle, show marks of great antiquity. While the fine old churches and cathedrals, with their tall spires, extending up into the clouds, bear evidence of its former grandeur. The old Rathhaus Church, is a noble specimen of the architectural skill, of past ages, and according to the date on its walls, was dedicated in the year 1280. Its main chapel, is three hundred and eighty feet long, one hundred and sixty wide, and one hundred and thirty-four feet between the floor and ceiling. It contains many fine works of art, with a beautiful marble altar seventy feet high, and three large organs, one of which has five thousand pipes.

In the south wing of this church, occupying four sides

of a large room, is to be seen the great picture, which was painted over four hundred years ago, and called the Dance of Death. This picture consists of a large number of life size figures, representing various classes of people, from the peasant, to the pope, or emperor, and by the side of each, is a skeleton, representing death. At the head of this group, is death playing on a flute, then comes a farmer in full vigor of life, next a lawyer, a priest, a warrior, a politician, a king, or emperor, and the man and woman of pleasure, as well as people in almost every condition of life. Between each of these figures, is the skeleton death, dancing a jig, and grinning in the most hideous manner, while he is holding on to the arm of his victim, and pulling them along. The woe-begone expression of the victim, and the fiendish grin of death, will impress itself so firmly on the mind of the beholder, that he never can forget it.

In the Rathhaus Church, is the wonderful clock so often referred to, by writers on mechanism. This clock has many dials, on which are represented the whole system of astronomy, the sun, moon and planets, also the day of the week, month and year. The twelve signs of the Zodiac, are represented by figures of animals, like the old fashioned almanacs. At twelve o'clock each day, the great bell strikes the hour, the chime bells ring, the organ plays a tune, and two life-like figures come out of the clock, and bow to the audience. The great dial, six feet in diameter, turns on its axis; a hand points to the day of the week, month and year, and the changes of the moon are shown, with various things relating to the solar system.

DENMARK.

It was with feeling of regret, that I left Lubeck, a city containing so many relics of antiquity, and so much identified with the history of past ages. Having parted with my company here, I took passage on a Baltic steamer, where no one spoke, or understood the English language. I found myself, a stranger in a strange land, and for the first time, I felt like turning back. I had for some time been accustomed to hearing the French, Flemish, Dutch, and German spoken, but now for the first time, I heard the Danish, which added a new link to my already confused ideas of foreign language.

The country along the south end of the Baltic Sea, is level; some places the land rises only a few feet above the water. In places, trees and farm houses, are seen from the deck of the steamer, but at other points nothing was visible above the horizon. The water of the Baltic is but little salt, almost without tide, and its commerce is very extensive. At one view, I counted, one hundred and twenty-eight vessels, with their canvass all spread making the finest display of shipping that I had ever seen.

The land in Denmark, is mostly level, full of small lakes, and sand knolls. The land is not rich, but is under a high state of cultivation, producing all kinds of grain common to northern Europe. There are many artifical groves, consisting of pine and beech trees, but they appear to be more for ornament, than use, as the timber used here, principally comes from Norway, and the coal from England. Peat is found on almost every farm, and large ricks of it are seen drying for winter use. There is no fencing in this country, and horses, cattle and sheep, are tied with a long rope while feeding on the pastures.

In the north part of the Island of Zealand, I was surprised at the great length of the days in midsummer. In addition to its high northern latitude, the reflection of the sun on the water, makes long twilight, morning and evening, and it was not dark, until eleven o'clock at night, while daylight begins to appear at one o'clock in the morning. In traveling through this country at ten o'clock in the evening, I found houses closed, and people retired for the night, while it was still daylight.

Thirty-eight miles down the coast from Copenhagen, is located the old city of Elsinore, with its narrow streets, dirty alleys, and rough paved streets, but containing nothing to interest a stranger. The surroundings of this city, are very beautiful, and it is said to be the most attractive place in Denmark. North of the city, on an elevated point of land, extending out into the sound, stands the great fortress of Cronborg, which was built about three hundred years ago. This castle, is a magnificent structure, built of red granite, of a gothic style of architecture, and is considered the finest castle in northern Europe. Its position is very beautiful, being surrounded by a fine park, containing paved walks and driveways, and overlooks the sound, which its guns command. The castle is surrounded by two walls, and two moats, and contains a chapel, a museum, a theatre, and is garrisoned by one thousand soldiers. It was on the terrace of its walls, (according to Shakespeare), Hamlet met the ghost of his father; the exact spot where the meeting occurred, was pointed out by our guide.

The channel at this point, connecting the Baltic with the North Sea, is only two miles wide, and it was at this place, the Danes for many years levied tribute on all vessels, passing into the Baltic Sea.

One mile from Cronborg Castle, on the beach of the sound, is a number of bath houses, and hotels, and people from different parts of Denmark, collect here during the summer season, making it a Newport, or Saratoga. Back from these bath houses, in a beautiful park, stands the Royal Chateau, formally the country residence of the king of Denmark. It is no longer the dwelling place of royalty, but is occupied by private parties, who keep it open to the public. As we entered this palace, tickets were handed us, for which we paid two marks each, after which we were conducted up four flights of stairs, the last one, opening into a fine shady garden. Here we had an excellent view of the sound, as well as the Swedish coast for many miles, including the old city of Helsingborg, with its old fashioned church steeples, and red tile roof houses. In the back part of this garden, we were shown the grave of Hamlet, Prince of Denmark, whose memory has been immortalized by Shakespeare's tragedy. Around this grave, is a circular knoll, and in the center of which, rises a round marble shaft, of some twelve feet in hight, being the only monument erected to the memory of the departed Prince.

COPENHAGEN.

The capital of Denmark, is built on an arm of sea, which extends back some ways from the sound, and forming an excellent harbor. The sound at this point connecting with the Swedish coast, is eighteen miles wide, and through it, all the vessels pass, entering the Baltic. Copenhagen is built on level land, which rises only a few feet above the water, and by numerous canals the commerce is brought into the heart of the city. The city is surrounded by a high wall, on the outside of which is a moat one hundred feet wide, filled with water, and crossed by drawbridges. The city is well fortified, having many forts, or battlements around its walls, besides three large forts, built out in the sound.

Here is a large navy harbor, containing the Danish fleet with many old three deckers, that have achieved victories, more than one hundred·years ago, and here also, are many iron clad ships, of the latest model. The streets of Copenhagen, are mostly wide, the houses high, built of gray stone. The city contains many fine parks, and 130,000 inhabitants. Here are many elegant public buildings, the most remarkable of which, is the Savior's

Church, containing a tower, two hundred and ninety feet high, and ascended by winding stairs, on the outside A view from this tower, is very picturesque overlooking the city, with its many parks, canals, forts and harbors; and the Swedish coast far in the distance. Among the many curiosities of the city, is the exchange palace, with its singular spire, representing in its formation, four dragons, with their tails twisted together, and tapering upwards, after the fashion of a corkscrew, while their heads are turned downwards, and standing out so as to represent the four points of the compass.

The royal park is said to be among the finest in Europe, containing large trees, between which are flower gardens, beautiful walks, and fountains. The singing of birds, and chattering of squirrels, might cause a person to imagine himself in a native forest, instead of being in the heart of a populous city.

Outside of the city walls, is located the Trivoli gardens, which is a great place of resort for people of all classes, which is to Copenhagen, what the Champs Elysees is to Paris. Here are theatres, menageries, museums, bowling alleys, circuses, and numerous cafes, supplied with bands of music, making it the gayest place in Denmark.

Copenhagen is the only place in Europe, where I saw the horse cars in general use. Here are many lines running to different parts of the city, carrying as many passengers on the tops of the cars, as in the inside, and all for two cents apiece.

CHAPTER VI.

MISTAKEN IDENTITY.

While at my hotel in Copenhagen, I was called on by two gentlemen, who wished to see me on business; one of whom was an editor of a daily paper, and the other a banker. Through an interpreter, they explained the object of their visit, by saying, that they were operating extensively in United States bonds, and wished my opinion with regard to repudiation. In reply, I told them that the United States was a large country, with immense resources, and all its debts would undoubtedly be paid in full. In answer to this opinion, they referred to some things in government affairs, which I was unacquainted with, and felt almost ashamed to acknowledged my ignorance of these matters. But I apologized by saying: that I was not a politician, consequently was not well posted in political affairs. They next asked me if I had not been Governor General of Illinois. I replied that I was a farmer, and never had held office, but there was a man whose name sounded like mine, that had been govenor of the state. After asking a few other questions, they picked up their hats, and making low bows departed.

Next morning the clerk of the hotel, read and explained to me a long editorial in the morning paper, in which the editor stated, that ex-governor general M——. of Illinois, U. S., was stopping at hotel Phœnix. and having called on him, obtained some items, relating to American affairs. In this article he gave a full discription of my personal appearance, and supposed political acts, not forgetting to state that I had stolen two hundred and twenty-three thousand dollars, from the state, besides making an attempt to rob the general government out of a large amount. And being detected in these robberies, caused me to deny my identity, claiming always to have been a private citizen. and closing the article by comparing my case to that of General Arnold, when traveling through France.

I did not feel myself much flattered by this newspaper article, besides it did me a great injury, as it pointed me out to the hordes of beggars, who infest the city, and fall on every tourist, who is supposed to have plenty of money. Next day, on leaving the hotel, I found at the door, a crowd of beggars, of all ages, and sexes, all of whom, were clamorous for money. I made an effort to pass them by, but this was not easily done. as they followed me for some ways, with their old dirty hats run into my face. One old man addressed himself to me, in an earnest manner, making rapid jestures with his bare, skeleton-looking arms, which were thrust almost into my face. I inquired of my guide what the old man was saying. He replied: "that I was a stingy cuss, after having stolen seven million dollars from my government, now refuse to give a poor beggar a penny."

SWEDEN.

After spending sometime in Denmark, I crossed the sound, and made a short tour through Sweden. The country through which I traveled, is generally level, with occasional hills covered with stone and gravel, and with some marshes, and small lakes. The land naturally is not rich, but some of it is made so, by artificial means, and produces fine crops.

North of Helsingborg, along the straits, there is a range of mountains, or high hills, which contain neither timber nor vegetation of any kind.

Malmo is an old seaport, with a good harbor, and considerable commerce; and lines of steamers run from here to different cities on the Baltic.

The Swedes and Danes, have frequently been styled, the French of the North, on account of their easy manners, and politeness to strangers. A person travel-ing through these countries, must notice this charac-teristic among the people. Whatever tourists may think of the climate and soil, they must admire the politeness of its citizens.

PRUSSIA.

At Malmo, Sweden, we went aboard of a steamer for the southern coast of the Baltic, and one hundred and forty miles sail, brought us to Stralsund, Prussia, which is situated on the straits of Gellen. This city contains about 25,000 inhabitants, and has an ancient appearance with many fine old buildings, among which are two churches, which were built in the twelfth century. Stralsund is of no great commercial importance, but it has figured extensively in the different wars of Europe, and many a bloody battle has been fought over its walls. It is strongly fortified, being surrounded with two walls, and two moats, and is styled the Gibraltar of the Baltic.

The country in the north part of Prussia is level, with many small lakes and marshes; in some places the soil is light, with sandy knolls and barren flats. Wheat, rye, oats and barley, are the principal productions, of the country and it has frequently been styled the granary of Europe. There are many artificial groves in this country, some of which are very beautiful, and show what a large amount of timber can be raised on a small piece of ground. When a tract of land is worn out, and becomes unproductive, it is planted out with trees, and turned into a forest. These groves can be seen in all stages from one year, to one hundred years standing. The trees in these groves are mostly pine, planted about ten feet apart, and they grow tall and straight, sometimes eighty or ninety feet without limbs. At a proper time the timber is cut off, and the roots taken out, when the land is again put under cultivation.

Much of the farm work in this country, is done by women. I have frequently seen them plowing, mowing,

J

cutting grain, etc. In one place, I saw fifty or sixty women, engaged on an excavation for a railroad, while their overseer, a foppish looking man, wearing white kid gloves, with a cigar in his mouth, was walking around giving directions to them. It is very common here for women to hire out by the day or month, to work on a farm, while their husbands, and sons are serving in the army.

BERLIN.

The capital of Prussia, is built on a level sandy plain, and is one of the largest cities in Europe, containing over an half million inhabitants. The streets are mostly wide and straight, with houses constructed in the modern style of architecture, which gives to the city a strong resemblance to Philadelphia. The great avenue called Under the Linden, extending from the Royal Palace, to the Brandenburg Gate, is a beautiful promenade, adorned with shade trees, and along it are the best stores in the city.

The river Spree runs through the middle of the city, and connected with it, are numerous canals which conduct the commerce into different parts. The Royal Palace is situated near the heart of the city, and for elegance and grandeur, far exceeds any of the Royal Palaces that I have visited in Europe. The Royal family were at their summer residence, and the palace was open to the inspection of the public. In order to be admitted, we had to procure tickets from an officer of the royal staff, and have our names registered in a book; canes and umberellas etc., were deposited, and checks given for them, cloth slippers were furnished us to draw over our boots. After going through the trying ordeal of visiting a number of offices where our names were signed and countersigned, a conductor took us through seventeen apartments of the palace, and things of interest were pointed out. In the crown and jewel rooms, are many things of great value, composed of massive gold, set off with wreaths of diamonds. Here we saw the punch bowl of Frederick the Great, made of solid silver, and holding fifty-two gallons. In this bowl, the great monarch kept his beer.

DRESDEN.

One hundred and thirty miles from Berlin, we came to the fine old city of Dresden, the capital of the kingdom of Saxony. The city is built on both sides of the river Elbe, over which are two beautiful stone bridges, one fourth of a mile in length. Dresden contains a population of 130,000, and is well built with many wide streets bordered by high stone houses, which have a white, clean, appearance. It has many fine public buildings, with beautiful parks, squares and pleasure grounds, and is a favorite residence for English and American travelers, who prolong their stay on the Continent. By them, it is styled the Florence of the North, on account of its good hotels, cheap living, and its fine works of art.

The museum of Dresden, is among the largest in

Europe, and occupies all sides of a public square. The armory department at this museum is the largest and finest in the world, far exceeding the Tower of London. Here arms and trophies of war, that belonged· to the middle ages, are collected, and exhibited to the public. Life-size figures representing kings and great warriors, are seated on horseback, clothed in their armor, and holding in their hand, the sword used by them in achieving their victories. While in this part of the museum, we met with an adventure, which came nigh being serious. The guide that conducted us through the museum, could speak no English, and his explanation was only valuable to those of the party who understood German; on this account one of our English companions refused to pay the usual fees. The conductor placed himself in the door, to prevent him from passing out, when our English friend threw him to one side, and in return the conductor drew a pistol and fired; the ball passed through the coat and vest, leaving a red mark on the skin under the Englishman's arm. This affair created a great excitement, and we found ourselves surrounded by a file of soldiers, and under arrest. The chief officer of the museum came with an interpreter, and when understanding the trouble, he furnished us with a guide who could converse in English, to show us again through the museum.

The carrying chairs, are much used in Dresden, and are very popular, being no more expensive than a cab. These chairs are nicely made with silk curtains that close up all around, and are caried by two men like the old fashioned hand-barrow. When a lady wishes to go to church or a ball, she sends for one of these chairs, and is carried there and back, by men who make this their business.

Near the city is the field of the great battle of October 1813, fought by Napolean against the allies, and here is a monument built of red granite, to the memory of Moreau, on the spot where he fell.

From Dresden we ascended the Elbe, in a small steamer, and made a short tour through Austria, stopping on our return at Saxon Switzerland. This place so much spoken of by tourists, consists of mountain scenery, with green valleys, and rocky cliffs, extending for some ways along the Elbe. But I think its beauty is much overrated.

GERMANY.

In the north part of Germany, especially in Hanover and Saxony, the country is level, but in the south and west part, it is divided between mountains and plains. There is no fencing in this country, consequently all kinds of stock are herded while feeding on pasture. But few farm houses are seen, as people live mostly in villages; in some cases, a long way from their farms. Public roads, seldom exceed twenty feet in width, and are all macadamized. Fruit or ornamental trees are planted on each side of the roads, which adds much to the beauty of the country. Coal and peat, are found in many places, but timber is scarce, and seldom met with except on the mountains, or artificial groves. Beets for the manufacture of sugar, are raised extensively, and also white poppies, for the production of opium.

The hotels in Germany, as well as those in other parts of the Continent, are kept on the restaurant plan, so that a person pays only for what he gets. Charges are made out in writing, and in some cases, enumerating each article of diet furnished, as well as lodging, service, candles, soap, etc., and the waiters always expect fees in addition to these charges. In some places a traveler is surprised to find two bills to pay, one at the office of the hotel, and the other at the office of the restaurant.

The cities of Germany, like other countries of Europe differ in many things from those of the United States. Here people of various stations in life, as well as occupations, are mostly known by their dress. Clergymen, hackmen, students at college, waiters at hotels, wash-women and flower girls, are dressed in uniform. In hotels or restaurants, women are never seen waiting on the table, but in many places, especially in France, women are seen acting as clerks or cashiers. It is very common for people here to pay money for service rendered, let it be ever so light, such as changing money or giving information, and I have never met a person who would not accept money for service of this kind, if offered.

That part of Germany lately ceded to Prussia, is full of soldiers, and martial music is heard late and early on the streets of every city or town. This large army is supported by the people, on whom they are quartered, which causes a bad feeling towards the Government. In some cases people pay their army tax by taking soldiers in their house to board, who become part of their own family.

I have been surprised to see with what veneration the Germans hold the stork; it being regarded as a sacred bird, which no person would think of killing, or molesting in any way. These birds are quite tame, and are frequently seen following the plowman, or feeding with the chickens in the barnyards. The storks frequently build their nests on the top of chimneys which shows as large as a hogshead, and will continue to lay and hatch in the same nest for many years in succession. When a nest is commenced on a chimney top, the flue is stopped up, and no further use is made of it, as it would be an omen of bad luck to disturb them in any way.

A TOUR THROUGH GERMANY.

Seventy-one miles west of Dresden, we came to Leipsic, a city of some 80,000 inhabitants, and largely engaged in the book manufactory. Here are over two hundred book establishments, with three hundred steam printing presses, where papers, books, and magazines are printed in different languages to circulate all over Europe. The city is principally built of white stone, and is more flourishing than any other city that I visited in Germany.

Close by Leipsic is pointed out the great battlefield of

October, 1813, where the French army, under Napoleon, was defeated by the allies.

Two hundred and sixty-eight miles south-west of Leipsic we came to Frankfort-on-the-Main. The route between these points is very interesting, passing through parts of five German states, and through many old fortified cities, where the ruins of old feudal castles and towers, are still to be seen.

FRANKFORT-ON-THE-MAIN.

The city of Frankfort is situated on the north bank of the river Main, and on a level plain, which is of many miles in extent. The term, On-the-Main, is used to distinguish this city from Frankfort-on-the-Oder. The city contains a population of 100,000, and is of great antiquity, as its history dates back to the fourth century. For many centuries it was the capital of Germany, and here most of her Emperors were crowned. Frankfort is well built, with many wide streets, beautiful parks and squares, and contains a large number of fine old churches and palaces. In the Jewish part of the city, the streets are very narrow, and the houses are built projecting over into the streets. Each story above, projects out further than the one below, giving to the rooms above, an additional width. From the river the city has a beautiful appearance; the houses being mostly six stories high, built of white stone, and at a distance look like palaces of marble. The river Main is navigable at this point, and small steamboats run from here into the Rhine, twenty miles distant.

Frankfort formerly was one of the four independent cities of Germany, making its own laws, the same as other members of the Rhinish Confederacy. But it is now attached to Prussia, with five thousand Prussian soldiers quartered on it, for whom it is taxed to support. In no place, in all my travels, have I found so bitter feeling against the government as here. The city has not only lost its independence, but much of its wealth is taken to support a policy, with which it has no sympathy. Since its annexation to Prussia, it has suffered much in commerce, and public confidence, and no longer sustains that high position among the cities of Europe it once had.

HOMBURG.

Ten miles north of Frankfort, at the foot of the Taurus mountains is located the town of Homburg, much celebrated as a watering and gambling place. Here are fine springs of mineral water, and the grounds, around them are highly ornamented with shade trees, among which are fountains, artificial lakes, deer parks, beautiful walks, and drive ways. Each morning from six to eight o'clock, thousands of people collect around these springs to drink the water, which is dealt out in mugs by waiting girls, while a band consisting of sixty musicians play for the amusement of the people. During the watering season people from all parts of Europe collect here talking different languages, and representing a great variety of fashions and costumes.

K

Homburg belongs to gamblers, who organized themselves into a company some twenty-six years ago,
under a royal charter, building many fine hotels, and
large blocks of buildings, ornamenting the grounds,
sparing no money in making the place attractive.
They built the kursaal, (or gambling house) at the cost
of one million guilders, which for size and grandeur
compares favorably with many of the royal palaces of
Europe. This building contains many apartments,
consisting of gambling, dancing, and reading rooms,
all of which are furnished in the most extravagant
manner. The reading rooms, of which there are three
in number, are supplied with papers from many different
countries, and in a great variety of languages.

At ten o'clock each day the gambling commences,
and continues without any intermission, until eleven at
night. There are four apartments allotted to gambling,
each of which has a large table where the gamblers
are seated, and all persons having their pile of gold
or silver before them, with a rake to draw in the money
when they win. One man represents the bank, and
another the party playing, and between them the cards
are dealt, and it does not require more than a half
minute to decide the game, when the winning party
hauls in the money with their rake, putting it up again
for another chance. The bank always retains so many
chances in its favor, diminishing the chances of the
playing public. In addition to the forty-eight players
seated at each table, those looking on frequently throw
down money and take their chances. Some of the tables

use the roulette wheel, instead of cards, and women take part in the game, as well as men, and appear to have as much money.

RHINE VALLEY.

The valley of the Rhine in many places, is eight or ten miles in width, and is said to be unequalled in fertility by any other district of country in Europe. Farming land here, in most cases belongs to its occupants, and is very valuable, but is bought and sold to no great extent, being retained in families from one generation to another. The average rental of land here, is from ten to twelve dollars per acre, while laborers on a farm, seldom receive over twenty-five cents per day. There is much wealth among the people here, and many of the German stock and money agencies of the United States, have their origin along the Rhine. The river Rhine has even banks, a rapid currant, and its waters have a milky color, caused by the glaciers of Switzerland. Many lines of steamboats are running up and down the river, mostly loaded with passengers. Along the river there is almost one continuous village, while back towards the mountains, are many fine towns and cities. Having traveled several hundred miles in the Rhine valley, and visited many of its old cities, a few of which I shall mention.

At the foot of the mountains, five miles from the Rhine, is located the city of Weisbaden, formerly the capital of the Duchy of Nassau. This is the oldest watering place in Germany; its waters having been used for medicinal purposes, more than two thousand years ago. During the summer months, it is crowded with visitors, filling its thirty-five hotels to overflowing. The great boiling spring of Weisbaden, is near the center of the town, and its smoking waters are conveyed to many bath houses in its vicinity.

The kursaal here, contains the usual number of gambling, reading, dancing and banquet rooms, while the squares around it, are filled with shops of trade. Here are beautiful walks and driveways, with flower gardens, fountains of water, and artificial lakes, around which the band plays, while the people drink their beer, or indulge in their cigars.

The city of Mayence, lies on the west bank of the Rhine, and contains 40,000 inhabitants. It has an ancient appearance, with narrow streets, and dreary looking alleys. This city is strongly fortified, being surrounded by three walls, and is, at present, the head quarters of the Prussian army. Mayence, is said to be the oldest city on the Rhine, and was the capital of the Rhinish province, when the Romans held this country. Part of an old Roman aqueduct, built nineteen hundred years ago, is still standing, as well as the tomb or monument of Drusus, bearing date, B. C. 48. On a public square stands a monument to the memory of Guttenburg, the inventor of printing, this city being his native place.

The river here is crossed by a pontoon bridge, and also by a steam ferry boat. Standing out in the river, are sixteen floating mills, with their machinery moved by the current.

Twenty-six miles up the river from Mayence, is located the old city of Worms, which has been so often referred to by church historians. Its streets are narrow, with many of its houses running up to a pinnacle, exhibiting their red tile roofs, which look at a distance like a large number of brick kilns. Here is an old cathedral, which dates back to the eighth century, also many other buildings of great antiquity. In 1521, was held here, the memorable diet to settle church difficulties, and which was attended by prelates and crowned heads from various countries of Europe. At this diet Martin Luther pointed out the many errors of the Catholic Church, and vindicated the principles of church reform in the presence of those high in authority.

Opposite Worms is an island in the river where tradition says, the valiant Siegfried, killed the dragon. This romantic story, founded on Rhinish mythology, was believed by the ancient inhabitants of this country, and paintings representing this scene, said to be fifteen hundred years old, are seen in public galleries along the Rhine. I have seen in different parts of Germany, bronze and marble statuary of this wonderful scene, from a small toy, to life size, where the man, horse, and dragon, are of natural size.

HEIDELBERG,

Is built on the river Necker, close to the foot of the mountain, five miles from the Rhine, and is a place where tourists frequently stay some time, as living is cheap, and hotels good. The Heidelberg University, established here more than six hundred years ago, is said to be the best institution of learning in Germany. It is now attended by about seven hundred students, who go dressed in uniform, wearing a badge on their arm, which denotes their order. Above the city is a fish pond, where trout are propagated for the market, and can be seen in all stages, from the size of a minnow, to that of a large fish, weighing four or five pounds.

Back of the city is the old Heidelberg Castle, now in a state of ruins. It stands part way up the mountain, three hundred feet above the city, on a steep, rocky cliff where the walls of the outer fortification, below the castle, are two hundred feet high. The castle and grounds around it, occupy a number of acres, partly cut out of the rocks, and containing shady walks, passing through beautiful pleasure grounds. Here stone fountains continue to furnish water, although a century or more has passed away, since their use has been required. This castle which has figured so extensively in the history of the country, was built in the twelfth century, and occupied by different Electors of Palatine, it being a royal palace, as well as a fortification. It is built of red granite, showing much beauty in its construction, and on the outside of the walls of one of its palaces, are many life size statues of warriors and noblemen, belonging to past ages. But these fine palaces are now in a state of ruin, the walls are mostly standing, but trees and ivy, are growing among them, and are now the habitation of owls and bats. Over one hundred years ago, the French army, after a long seige took this castle, blew up one of its towers and otherwise damaged it. Soon after this, the Elector of Palatine became King of Bavaria, and moved his residence to Munich, and the castle was abandoned to its fate.

In the cellar of one of the towers, is still to be seen the great wine tub, twenty-three feet in diameter, and twenty-six feet high, with staves nine inches thick. Every year this big cask was filled with wine from the Electors own vineyard, although a century or more has passed since it was used, it still appears in a good state of preservation.

BADEN BADEN.

The chief of watering places, is situated in a valley surrounded by mountains or hills, of the Black Forest, and about eight miles from the Rhine. Passing through the city is a small stream, called Oos, the bottom of which is flaged with flat stone, and its banks are walled up to the level of the street, and houses built thereon. The valley of the Oos, is narrow, and part of the city is built on the side-hill, rising one street above another, which gives to the place a picturesque appearance. Along the valley, as well as on the hillside, are many beautiful residences, surrounded by green meadows and flower gardens, through which are paved walks, and driveways.

Baden Baden, is the most fashionable watering place in Europe, and here are collected during the summer season, kings and dukes, with other sprigs of nobility, as well as the gay and fashionable people from different countries, speaking a great variety of languages. Although the city contains but a few thousand inhabitants, it has some of the finest hotels in Europe, and during the summer months, are quartered here, from twenty to thirty thousand strangers whose principal amusements are gambling, and horse racing.

There are many springs here of different temperature, and containing various grades of mineral water. The great boiling spring is 168° Farrenheit, so hot as to scald a person's hand, if held in the water. A large bath house stands over this spring, and the water from it is conducted to other bath houses in the vicinity. The water for drinking purposes, flows out of a marble tank in the pump house, and every morning from five to six o'clock, crowds of people call here to drink the water while the band plays, always commencing with the morning hymn.

Each morning large flocks of goats are driven in from the country, and the milk from them is drank warm. Close by here, is a goat house, where milking is going on, and people drinking it from the mug of the milkmaid, at all hours of the day.

The Conversation House, or kursaal is an extensive building, five hundred and twenty feet in length, and adorned by a Corinthian portico in front. It contains many apartments, furnished in the most extravagant manner, and known as ball, lecture, banquet, reading, and gambling rooms. Around the kursaal, are beautiful pleasure grounds, shaded with trees, lighted with gas, and supplied with seats. Every evening, many thousand people collect here to listen to the music, as they drink their beer, or sup their coffee, while the fashionably dressed ladies and gentlemen, are promenading back and forth. The avenues leading through these grounds, are fitted up with bazars, or stalls of traders, from Frankfort, Paris, and Switzerland.

According to history, Baden Baden, has been a watering place for more than eighteen hundred years. Underground baths are still to be seen, which are said to have been built by the Romans, when they possessed this country. But it has become celebrated within the last century, when gambling was introduced, and people collected here from all parts of Europe, to try their luck at the tables. Much of the money obtained from visitors has been expended in ornamenting, and beautifying the place, so as to make it attractive to strangers. The streets are supplied with fountain pumps, some of which send forth cold, and others hot water. Public baths are built, where the poor can bathe free of charge, and here is a molkin, or whey cure, to which the poor invalid can have access. The gamblers pay yearly for the use of the buildings, and privilege of gambling, three hundred thousand florins to the city, and a like amount to the government of Baden, which almost relieves the people from taxation. In addition to this, they pay a band of sixty musicians, to play for the public, as well as

L

policemen to guard the place, and men to wait on visitors. There appears to be no odium attached to public gambling; here, it being a legitimate business, but private gambling is considered disreputable, and parties engaged in it are liable to a fine.

The Catholic Collegate Church here, is a fine specimen of antiquity, built in the tenth century, and contains many monuments and statues, to the memory of warriors and divines of past ages. Among the most remarkable of its contents, are the remains of a priest lying in state. The bones are put together with gold wire, and the skeleton adorned with gold lace, containing many jewels with diamond sets, and the whole is enclosed in a glass case, which stands on a marble platform near the altar. For more than three hundred years, the remains of this old priest have lain here, and on account of his goodness and piety, the church intends to keep him until the judgment day.

SURROUNDINGS OF BADEN BADEN.

On the top of a mountain above the city are the ruins of Hokenbaden Castle, which was built in the tenth century, and occupied in turn by different dukes of Baden. About two hundred years ago, it was taken by the French army, and some of its towers blown up; but a small portion of it has been restored, and occupied by parties who keep a restaurant and beer garden, for the accommodation of visitors. The walls of this castle unlike those of Heidelberg Castle, are rough, and show but little skill in their construction. Portions of the walls have fallen down, and large size trees have grown up between them. The highest part now standing is the tower of Knights Temple, being one hundred and fifty feet high, and at an elevation of two thousand and seventy feet above the Rhine valley. A view from the top of these walls is very fine; below us, was the great Rhine valley, eight miles wide, spread out like a map with its numerous towns and cities, and farming villages almost without number. Under the castle, are many apartments cut out of the native rock, which can be entered only with the assistance of a guide, carrying lights. These vaults were used in former times as a prison, where have been enacted many deeds of horror.

Overlooking Baden Baden, but in a different direction, is Mt. Mercury, on the top of which stands a stone tower, two hundred and twenty-five feet high. Near this tower is an image, in the form of a human being, cut out of stone, and dedicated to the god Mercury. But little is known of the history of this image. Tradition says it was erected over two thousand years ago, by a heathen nobleman who was restored to health at these springs. On the image there is an inscription reading thus: "To the God of Mercury, Curious, the the merchant, hath erected this, in fulfillment of his vow, because of restored health."

Above the city, reached by three hundred and sixty-two stone steps, stands the royal palace, the summer residence of the Grand Duke of Baden. Under this palace are many vaulted chambers cut out of the native rock, and used as prisons, during the twelfth and thirteenth centuries, being the head quarters of the Roman inquisition for this part of Germany. An account of many bloody tragedies, which took place here, are given in the book of martyrs, with which many of the readers are familiar. Each one of our party being provided with lights, preceded by our guide, we commenced a descent into these underground vaults. Here we found apartments guarded by stone doors, ten or twelve inches thick, which as they turned on their hinges with a grating noise, almost made me shudder. At last we came to the center of the prison, and on looking up eighty-five feet, as if from a well, we could see the light of day. Passing through a number of rooms, we came to the mouth of a subterranean passage, one and a half miles in length, connecting with the castle on the mountain. Through this passage, heretics were brought to be tried, and executed. Next we came to a large room, with niches in the walls, to receive lamps. This was the court room, where prisoners were tried, and from which there is a passage leading to the place of execution. At the end of this passage, there is a recess in the wall, where the Virgin Mary stood. The prisoner having been found guilty, was ordered to kiss the Virgin, when her iron arms would open to embrace him, and the many knives in her metalic mantle would cut him in peices; at the same time, a trap-door would open for the victim to fall through, to where a current of water would wash off the remains. In some of the rooms are hooks and staples

where implements of torture were fastened. Hundreds
of victims were brought in at night, imprisoned, tried,
and executed in these underground vaults, while the
outside world would know nothing of it.

Two miles from Baden Baden, in the valley of the
Oos, is the convent of Lichenthal, a place famous in
church history, and known during the thirty years war,
as the stronghold of Catholicism. In one of the old
churches here, are the skeletons of two females, kept in
glass cases on each side of the altar. These remains
are decorated with jewels and diamonds, with many
gold rings on the fingers and toes. One of these relics
is of a woman, who founded the church, and died in the
year 1260.

After a stay of ten days in Baden Baden, we left it
and made a short tour through the Black Forest, after
which we crossed the Rhine, and visited Strasburg,
France.

CHAPTER VII.

This is an old, and strongly fortified city on the French frontier, being separated from Germany, by the river Rhine, and contains a population of 83,000. It was in this city that Louis Napoleon (now Napoleon III.), made a bold attempt to obtain the throne of France. The prison where he was confined, was pointed out, and the manner of his escape explained.

Here in Strasburg is a large cathedral containing a remarkable spire which has long been the admiration of the world. This spire of this cathedral is the highest in the world, being four hundred and seventy -four feet above the pavement, being constructed of red granite, beautifully carved, and at a distance has the appearance of lace work. In one wing of the cathedral, stands the astronomical clock, so much spoken of by travelers, and which is considered by many, to be the greatest piece of mechanism in the world. This clock stands on the floor, and is sixty feet high, the top of which is reached by a long flight of winding stairs. By the side of the clock is a tower of equal hight, on the top of which stands a mammoth bronze chicken cock, with its head and tail erect.

At twelve o'clock each day, a number of figures of men and women comes out of the clock, one of whom strikes a bell, giving the hour, after which a life size figure appears representing Christ, and holding before him a cross. Then comes twelve other life size figures, representing the Apostles, who march by Christ. Each one stops and bows, as he passes, which acknowledgement of obedience Christ returns by the waving of his right hand. At the same time, the chicken cock flops his wings, and crows three times, after which the great organ plays a tune. This clock, like the one at Lubeck shows the revolutions of the heavenly bodies, day of the week, month, and year, changes of the moon, signs of the zodiac etc., all of which are shown on large dials. Large crowds of people collect here daily to see the performance.

A TOUR THROUGH SWITZERLAND.

After leaving Strasburg we went ninety miles up the Rhine, the valley of which is from six to eight miles in width, and densely populated. Along the road we passed through many old towns, containing ruined castles and fortifications, the relics of past ages, which gives to the country a feudal aspect. On this road is the old town of St. Louis, much celebrated for its fish culture, where a large amount of fish eggs or ovas are collected for distribution in the different lakes and rivers of Europe.

In the north west corner of Switzerland is located the city of Bale, which is built on both sides of the Rhine, whose light green floods run by with great rapidity. This city is well built with many wide streets, or boulevards, containing shade trees, fountain pumps, and also many public squares, parks, and flower gardens. There are a number of large paper, and ribbon factories here, and from this source the city has derived much of its wealth. The signs on business houses mostly have two inscriptions, one in French, and the other in German, as both of these languages are spoken.

Four miles above Bale is to be seen a monument on the battle field of St. Jacob, which was erected to the memory of sixteen hundred Swiss soldiers, who fought for ten hours, fifteen thousand French, lead by Louis XI. History says only ten of the Swiss escaped death, all the rest being left dead on the field, along with twice this number of foes whom they had slain.

From Bale, the railroad follows up the valley of the Rhine for some miles, then it leaves it and takes to the mountain, along deep gorges, rocky hill sides, through tunnels, and crossing frightful chasms, by iron viaducts. The scenery on the road becomes more rugged and wild, the mountains rocky, and destitute of vegetation. At last, we saw in the distance the range of Barnese Alps with their high peaks covered with snow, at the sight of which, some of our traveling companions became wild with enthusiasm, manifesting as much joy as Pizaro did, when he first discovered the snowy cliffs of the Andes. At Lake Sampach, which is a small Swiss lake, we saw the monument erected on the battle-field where Leopold, Prince of Austria, and many of his nobles were slain, and thereby the independence of Switzerland established. At the end of the railroad, we came to the city of Lucern, and thus closed our first days travel among the Alps.

LAKE LUCERN AND SURROUNDINGS.

Lake Lucern is said to be the most beautiful of all the lakes of Switzerland, and along its shores are many old towns, which have figured extensively in the early history of the country. This lake is twenty-seven miles long, averaging two in breadth, with wings at each side, in the shape of a cross, and has three lines of small steamboats, running to different towns on its shore. On both sides of the lake the mountains rise many thousand feet above its waters, with here and there a high peak covered with perpetual snow. In some places, pine trees, and grass grow high up on the mountain, and its slopes are dotted over with houses of peasants who obtain their living mostly by selling butter and cheese made of goats milk. From Baunnen to Fluelen a distance of twelve miles, there is a carriage road along the lake, which is cut out of the rocky cliff, through many tunnels, and across viaducts.

M

Two miles above the head of the lake, we came to the old town of Altorf which has became famous on account of its connection with William Tell, and on that account it is visited by almost every person, traveling through the Alps. This town is situated in a narrow valley, with high mountains rising almost perpendicularly on either side, and their tops covered with perpetual snow. Trees are left standing at the base of the mountain, to protect the town from avalanches and falling rocks, which have been so destructive to many of the Swiss towns.

One and a half miles above the town, on the bank of a creek is a small chapel, which was built to m ark the spot where Tell lived and died.

Many people in the United States regard the history of Tell as fictitious, and founded on tradition, which has been made famous by the writers of romance. But there is no foundation for this opinion, as these events occurred at the commencement of the Swiss revolution, which terminated in the independence of the country. All these events entered into history at the time, and the place where they occurred, were ·marked, and held sacred by the people to this day. On a public square at Altorf, stands the colossal statue of Tell, occupying the spot where he stood when he shot the apple off his son's head. This statue represents Tell, with one hand resting on his bow, while the other hand holds aloft an arrow, with this inscription: "This arrow was intended for thee, tyrant Gesler, if I had killed my son." One hundred and seventeen yards from this statue, is a monument sixty feet high, built on the place where the boy stood when the arrow split the apple on his head, and close by it is a fountain, occupying the spot where grew the linden tree on which Gesler's hat was placed, for all men to do obeisance to it as they passed.

Seven miles down the lake from Fluelen, is to be seen Tell's Chapel, built on a rock at the water's edge, and reached from the land side, by steps cut in the rocky cliff above. This is the place where Tell escaped from his captors, as he was being conveyed a prisoner to Kussnacht. History says the night was dark and stormy, and the vessel was in danger of being dashed to pieces against the rocks, when all on board would have perished. They having great faith in Tell's skill to manage the vassel, untied him, when he ran the boat ashore, killed the tyrant Gesler, jumped off on this rock and thus made his escape. This chapel was built thirty years after Tell's death, and dedicated in the presence of one hundred and twenty men, who knew him well, and whose names now appear on its walls.

Two miles below Tell's chapel, on the opposite side of the lake, was pointed out a table rock, seven hundred feet above the water. This is said to be the place where the patriots met on the night of the 7th, of November, 1307, and bound themselves by an oath to free their country. Tell, it is said, was on his way to attend this meeting, when he was taken prisoner at Altorf.

On the east side of the Lake, is the Rigi, a mountain

of great celebrity, on account of its isolated position. being partly surrounded by lakes, which makes it a natural observatory. The view of sunrise, from the summit of this mountain, is said to be very beautiful, and crowds of people ascend it the day before, staying all night, in order to enjoy this view. But a large majority of whom meet with disapointment, as the mountain is often enveloped in clouds. From Lucerne, the Rigi is in plain view, and looks as though it could be reached in an hour's walk, but to reach its summit requires fifteen miles travel. Seven miles by steamboat, and eight miles on foot. Women sometimes ride a mule, up the mountain, while others are carried by two men, in a carrying chair. A large number of men are engaged in this business, and will carry a person eight miles up the mountain, for fifteen francs. On the top of the Rigi, there are two hotels to accommodate visitors, and everything used in them, as well as the materials for their construction, were carried upon the backs of mountaineer's. At Kussnacht, which is at the foot of the Rigi, is still to be seen the ruin of Gesler's Castle, and here was the head quarters of the Austrian army, when they held Switzerland.

On the morning of the ninth of August, I accompanied a party of seventeen Americans, in making an ascent of the Rigi. The day was fine, without a cloud in the horizon, and the view from the summit of the mountain was grand beyond discription. To the south, and surrounding two sides of the base of the mountain lay the clear blue waters of lake Lucerne, at the north, lies lake Zug, while in the distance, could be seen the snow-capped peaks of the Barnes Oberlands. North-east of us on the opposite side of the valley, is the Ross-berg, from whose slope came the great land slide of 1806. This land slide was the largest, and most fatal, of any known among the Alps. The ground for over two miles in length gave way, filling up the valley to a great depth, with dirt and rocks, distroying three villages, and killing four hundred and fifty-five persons.

CITY OF LUCERNE.

The city of Lucerne is situated at the foot of lake Lucerne, and is divided by the river Reuss, which runs from the lake with great rapidity, and over which are many bridges. The location of Lucerne is of matchless beauty, with the deep blue waters of the lake in front, Mt. Pilatus on the right, and Mt. Rigi on the left, while far in the distance are seen the snow-capped peaks of the Engelberg mountains. The end of. the lake, here, is circular. The city is built on its banks, where the land rises only a few feet above the water, and is partly surrounded by an old wall with watch towers, now in a state of ruin. The city contains many fine hotels, with comforts and conveniences, seldom met in Europe, and also two old churches of great antiquity. Lucerne contains a population of 13,000, and is full of strangers during the summer months, as it is a great place of resort, for persons traveling among the Alps. During my stay in the city, Queen Victoria, and suit were here, and occupied all of a large hotel on the hill.

While here in Lucerne, I had my hair cut by a barber, and I gave him a franc, demanding my change back, but he refused to give me any. I pointed to his advertisement which read thus: "Cutting hair, half franc." He said that sign was for Swiss. "Americans much money, one franc." I tried to convince him that it required no more time to cut an American's hair, than that of a Swiss, but this argument had no effect.

BRUNING PASS.

At the ringing of the steamer's bell, crowds of people left their hotels in Lucerne, for a passage up the lake. Women with jocky hats, short dresses, and carrying in their hand, a long Alpine staff, were seen hurrying to and fro, full of life, animated with a prospect of a tramp among the glaciers.

Thirteen miles up the lake, we came to the village of Alpnach, a place of great antiquity, and surrounded by high mountains. Here are the remains of an old timber slide, used about fifty years ago, to convey timber from the mountains, into the lake. This slide was constructed of timbers, eight miles long, six feet wide, and four feet high, kept wet by a rill to diminish friction. Trees one hundred feet long, and four feet in diameter, would pass through this slide into the lake below, and from there, they were floated down the river Reuss, into the Rhine, where they were formed into rafts, to be sold in Holland.

At Alpnach, we left the steamer, for a diligence, and commenced our tour through the Bruning Pass, which is forty miles in length, passing over a high mountain and sometimes by the side of frightful precipices. But the road is good, and a large number of people pass it daily. Sometimes eight or ten coaches would follow each other in close succession, beside footmen without number.

On this road, are a number of small lakes, surrounded with rich meadows, while above them rise rocky crags, many thousand feet in hight. One of these crags was pointed out to us, as the place where an eagle many years ago, carried a child to its nest, high up on the cliff. This thrilling story runs thus: A woman while working in the meadow, left her infant a few weeks old, sleeping in a different part of the field, and on hearing it cry, looked up, and with horror, saw an eagle carrying it off. The alarm being given the villagers collected in large numbers, and means were provided for the child's rescue. A man was let down by a rope, from the top of the cliff, to the eagles nest, and thus rescued the child, restoring it again to its mother's arms, but badly wounded, from the claws of the eagle. As we passed these crags, we saw a number of eagles flying around them, and here they continue to build their nest, as in former times.

We stopped at Sarnen, which is an old Swiss town, at the foot of the lake, bearing the same name here, and visited an old church containing many relics of the Swiss revolution. In a glass case by the altar, is to be seen the remains of St. Nicholas, who died here in the year 1487. Within his ribs, where his heart once was

is a jeweled cross, with many other mementoes donated
by the Pope of Rome, to the departed saint.

While going up the mountain, women and children
followed us, in order to sell milk, fruit, and wooden
trinkets.   A troup of Swiss maidens, dressed in their
peculiar costume, consisting of a short dress, white
jacket, and a flat hat, accompanied us some ways up the
mountain, walking by the side of the coaches, and
singing mountain airs, the melody of which, could not
be surpassed by the Hutchinson family.

After a ride of twelve hours, we came to the town of
Brienz, situated at the head of lake Brienz, which is said
to be in the geographical center of Switzerland.   Here
we again went aboard of a steamer, on the lake, for
Giessback falls, and saw its three cascades, the highest
of which is over six hundred feet, of a perpendicular
fall.   Twelve miles sail down the lake, brought us to
Interlaken, a nice shady village, situated between lake
Brienz, and lake Thun, and containing a few thousand
inhabitants, and twenty-five hotels.   This is a place of
great attraction, and here tourists frequently stay a few
weeks.   Notwithstanding its large number of fine hotels,
people are frequently obliged to seek lodging in the
neighboring villages.   Here is a beautiful park with a
kursaal, containing reading rooms, and dancing halls,
where the band plays morning and evening, making it
the gayest place in Switzerland.   A tax is levied on all
strangers visiting Interlaken, for the support of this
kursaal, as well as the support of the poor of the canton,
a species of thieving that some people take exception to.

CHAPTER VIII.

In the United States, we have the White, Rocky, and Alleghany mountains, big rivers and lakes, as well as the great falls of Niagara, but no where on the Western Continent, can be found scenery to equal the mighty Alps. A person may read various accounts of these mountains, without forming a correct idea of their magnitude and grandeur, which can only be realized by seeing them.

Leaving our baggage at Interlaken, we took a carriage for Lauterbrunen, which is a small village ten miles south, and situated in a deep gorge of the mountain, where the sun does not shine until eleven o'clock in the morning. At this place the carriage road ends, and the tourist is obliged to continue his way on foot, or on horseback. Above the village is the Straubback falls, nine hundred feet high, being the highest waterfall in Europe, but the stream is small, and the water is reduced to spray, before it reaches the bottom.

N

South of the village of Lauterbrunen, is the Jung-frau, nearly three miles high, and covered with perpet-ual snow. I had seen this mountain at different times while traveling in Switzerland, sometimes while fifty or sixty miles away, and find that its grandeur increases by a closer view. On one side of the Jungfrau is the Wetterhorn, running up to a sharp peak, and of chalky whiteness; while on the other side is the Monch, which is called the giantess of the Oberlands, and is of equal whiteness. From a mountain opposite the Jung-frau, a fine view of it can be obtained, showing many square miles of snow and ice, with here and there a cliff of rocks, looking black and dreary, in contrast with the virgin whitness of the snow around them. We could see large cracks in the ice, some of which were ten or twenty feet wide, and one hundred or more deep, between which are crags of ice, like pyramids standing up in wild masses. High up on the mountain, we saw eight men walking in Indian file, one after the other, the guide going before, and slowly feeling his way with an Alpine staff. A rope was tied around the waist of each, and all fastened together, so if one should fall into a crevice in the ice, the others would support him. Frequently people are lost on this mountain, as large cracks are formed in the ice during the summer, which are covered over by snow in winter, and cannot be seen by the tourist. Baggage is left unclaimed at hotels in this vicinity, the owners of which are thought to have lost their lives among the glaciers.

While here we saw a number of avalanches from the

mountain, which were grand beyond description, while
the noise accompanying them, was like a continuous
discharge of artillery. These avalanches occur more or
less every warm afternoon, and at each discharge tons
of ice, accompanied by torrents of water are thrown
down from the mountain. High up on the glaciers
where the ice is many hundred feet in depth, a large cake
of it, which is of itself a mountain, would occasionally
break from its fastening, and commence a journey downwards, pitching over a cliff of rock two thousand feet
or more in hight, where it is broken into fragments,
and filling the air with mist. From here it continues
its way down the mountain, until it comes to another
high cliff of rocks, where it bounds over with a loud
roar as before; onward it continues in its wild career,
until it reaches the valley miles below. Amid the stillness of those Alpine solitudes, a report is heard which
reaches from mountain to mountain, succeeded by
another report, still louder, as though an earthquake
had taken place, or the mountain itself had fallen into
the valley. We may imagine the roar of Niagara, peals
of thunder, discharging of artillery, but these do not
equal the rumbling noise, or prolonged roar of a Jungfrau
avalanche.

While on this mountain we had the pleasure of wit-
nessing a scene of grandeur and sublimity seldom met
with, even by people who live among the Alps. Our
attention was first attracted by distant thunder, and on
looking toward lake Brienz, we saw a black cloud, not
high in the zenith, but on a level with us. This cloud

followed up the valley of Lauterbrunen, until it reached the mountain below us, and here it presented a scene of grandeur, which is beyond description. Above us, was shining the bright August sun, without a cloud in the sky, while below us, and almost under our feet, was a black thick cloud, from which came forth vivid lightning, heavy peals of thunder, and torrents of rain, drenching the valley below us, with floods of water.

A DANCE ON THE MOUNTAIN.

South of the village of Lauterbrunen, lies the Wengern Alps, which is separated from the Jungfrau, by a deep valley. On this mountain is a hotel, and high above it, is a rocky peak, where tourists frequently go to see the avalanches from the Jungfrau. On reaching this summit, we found there collected, a party of about twenty Americans of both sexes, some of whom were quite enthusiastic over the fine scenery, which was rendered more impressive by bottles of brandy, which they carried in their coat pockets. Among this party was Major General Snips of the late Southern Confederation, who was accompanied by a charming looking French lady, whom he called his wife, and toward whom he was very jealous of other men's attentions. The General is a man of remarkable personal appearance, being nearly seven feet high, slim and gaunt, with long ape-like arms which are all the while swinging back and forth, as though they were hung on hinges. No one of the party appeared to enjoy themselves so well, as the General.

He first made a speech, then sang a number of songs, among which were Old Uncle Ned, and Captain Jinks of the Horse Marines, then assisted by some of his companions, he closed the exercises with an old fashioned dance.

This dance was a very remarkable one, being on a smoth rock, many thousand feet above the valley, with no music but an accordeon in the hands of a tall lady in black, who pulled away on the instrument as though she was trying to tare it in twain. The General danced with all his might, twisting his long slim body into every possible position, while his feet were thrown around in all directions. Amid the roaring of the avalanches, the shrill squeakes of the accordeon, the loud laugh, and cheers of the bystanders, and above all these were heard the General's feet, rattling on the rock, first upon the heel tap, then upon the toe, with his long bony arms swinging to and fro, his gaunt form wriggling, while his long shaggy locks danced a jig. On, and on, went the dance, louder, and louder, were the shouts of the bystanders, and louder, and more offensive were the squeakes of the accordeon. But while in the hight of their merriment, a circumstance occured which broke up the dance, and destroyed the harmony of the party. By some means the General discovered one of the party, a red faced Yankee, making love to his wife. This he considered a Northern invasion of Southern rights, which honor bound him to correct, and he pitched into the Yankee, with true southern chivalry. The assault was vigorously contested, and blood ran freely, but through the interference of others, hostility ceased, peace was made, and the combatants, drank friends.

About two months after this occurrence, I met the General in Italy, when he informed me that his wife had run off with this same red faced Yankee, taking with her all his money and jewelry.

GRINDELWOLD.

Twelve miles south-east of Interlaken, in a deep valley, surrounded by snow-capped peaks, is located the village of Grindelwold. This place has been immortalized by the poems of Byron, and Shelley, on account of its wild scenery, and peculiar climate. Close by the village are two large glaciers, extending down into the valley, many thousand feet below the snow line, and from which comes forth large streams of water, equal to large creeks, with their turbid waters, roaring and foaming, as it pitches over rocks, on the way to the lake. These streams are formed by the melting of snow on the mountains, and run all summer without exhausing their source. At the foot of one of these glaciers is a cave cut into the ice, where men were at work, taking it out for shipment to Paris, and other cities of Europe. Farther up the mountain the ice rises like a perpendicular wall of nearly one hundred feet in hight. Here an enterprising Swiss has built a shanty on a rock, raised a flag, and cut a tunnel in the ice two hundred feet deep, lighted by lamps, and charges admittance fees. This tunnel has a remarkable appearance; the floor, roof,

and sides, being of pure crystal ice, shining in the lamp
light, like walls of diamonds, reminding one of the ice
palace, built by Queen Catherine of Russia.

The glaciers connected with Grindelwold, and Jungfrau, are said to be the most extensive ones of the Alps,
and the most dangerous to explore. I have conversed
with different guides, who make it their business to
conduct people across these glaciers. They say the
changes in them are but slight; crags of ice have stood
twenty or thirty years without any perceptible change,
except increasing in winter, and diminishing in summer.
The depth of the ice on these large glaciers, is not
known, but supposed in places to be, at least, fifteen
hundred feet. The line where vegetation ceases, and
snow is perpetual, differs very much on these mountains,
but it is said nine thousand feet above the level of the
sea is the average. In some places forests of pine, or fir,
are seen at a great hight, while at other places of equal
hight, are rocky cliffs, without vegetation of any kind.

After spending a few days among the Bernese Oberlands, climbing up rocky cliffs, and by the side of
frightful precipices, over crags of ice, and mountains of
snow, I felt willing to return to a more genial climate,
although highly delighted with my tour among the
glaciers.

On our way to Berne, we traveled on lake Thun,
which is a small lake of ten miles in length, by two in
breadth, and said to be eighteen hundred feet deep.
While steaming down this lake, our attention was
called to the surrounding scenery, which represents two

seasons of the year. On the lowlands the fields were green, with waiving grain, and blooming flowers, while beyond these are mountains covered with perpetual snow, showing both summer and winter, at one view.

BERNESE OBERLANDS.

The country in this part of the Alps, is very remarkable, but it would be impossible to give the reader a correct idea of it. Much of the country is wild, uninhabited, where the bear and chamois, roam undisturbed by human habitation; but where it is possible for a human being to live, the hardy mountaineers are found. The people here live in wooden houses of singular construction, lacking both beauty and convenience. Horses, plows or wagons, are seldom seen among the peasantry, the land being prepared for a crop by digging it with a hoe. Cattle, sheep, and goats, are herded off in the mountains, during the summer, and are seldom met with, in the inhabited part of the country. Wheat, oats, barley, and flax are raised, but are in small fields, which seldom exceed an half acre. In some places on the southern slope of the mountain, the land is terraced with stone walls, and vineyards, and fruit trees are seen, far above the valley. Manure for enriching the land, is carried up in baskets placed on women's heads, and the products of the land are carried down in the same way. Most of the farm work, is done by women, who are of a fine physical organization, many of whom cut off their hair yearly and sell it, as it is worth more in market, than women's hair of other countries. A young lady can sell her hair for money enough to buy her a wedding dress.

Travelers through the country are much annoyed, with women and children trying to sell them fruit, wooden trinkets, etc. Sometimes children will follow a carriage for miles up the mountain, with blocks of wood, to scotch the wheels; the girls singing songs, and the boys turning summersaults. The people are poor, and their children are beggars; the only wealth of the country belongs to hotel keepers.

In the deep gorge of the mountain, a man is sometimes found blowing an alpine horn, the sound re-echoing miles away, and coming back again, resembles a band of music. This alpine horn, which is so much celebrated among the Swiss, is a large wooden tube, six or eight feet in length, and when the atmosphere is right, its sound might be mistaken for Gabriel's trumpet.

BERNE.

The capital of Switzerland, has a population of 30,000, and is very singularly situated, being neither on a hill, nor in a valley, but on a table land, between the two. The river Aar, runs on three sides of it, and is crossed by two high stone bridges. The city is well built, with many wide streets, and high houses, principally constructed of white stone. Many of the business streets, have arcades on both sides of them, which are supported by massive columns, causing the sidewalk to pass under

o

the buildings. The streets and public squares, are well
supplied with fountains, many of which are ornamented
with colossal bronze figures of bears, the symbol of the
canton of Berne.

The capitol is a large stone edifice, without either
dome or cupola, but shows much skill and good taste
in its construction. The halls of senate and representa-
tives, are much like those at Washington, but not so
large and expensively furnished.

There are many curious things in Berne, among which
is the old clock tower, standing in the middle of one of
the principal streets. When this clock strikes, a
colossal bronze chicken cock flaps its wings, and crows
three times. Then a procession of bears come out of
the clock, and marches around the crowned figures of
Gog and Magog who gap, and lower their scepters at
each stroke of the bell.

At the east end of the city, there is a bear pit, where
a number of these animals are kept, for the amusement
of the public.

FROM BERNE TO GENEVA.

The country on the route between Berne and Lausanne,
a distance of eighty-five miles, is very hilly, and in some
places, mountainous, with here and there a fertile valley.
The land is very stony, with a yellow clay soil, but is
under a high state of cultivation, producing fine crops
of various kinds of grain. The plowing and teaming
are mostly done with cows, which are said to be more

serviceable than steers, besides supplying the family
with milk.

Twenty-two miles from Berne, we came to the old
city of Freiburg, a place famous in history, and known
during the Protestant wars, as the stronghold of Catholicism. This city is surrounded by a high wall, stretching
up hill and down, across deep gorges, and rocky knolls,
and ornamented with many watch towers, which make
the distant view of the city imposing, and highly
picturesque. Here is a great suspension bridge, over
the river Saarine, which for hight, and length of curve,
exceeds all other bridges in Europe.

The next place of interest on the road is Lausanne, a
city of some 22,000 inhabitants, and located on the
north bank of lake Geneva. This city is said to be the
dividing line between the French and German language.
The upper part of the city speaking French, while the
lower part speaks German.

At Lausanne, we went aboard of a steamer for Geneva,
thirty-five miles distant.

GENEVA.

This old and much celebrated city of the Alps, is
situated at the foot of Lake Geneva, and on both sides
of the river Rhone, where its blue waters rush by
with great rapidity. From the lake, the city has a
very imposing appearance, looking both large and grand,
and a person can scarcely credit the fact, that it only
contains 42,000 inhabitants. Fronting the lake, on

both sides of the river, are fine buildings, mostly six
stories high, constructed of white stone, and of a modern
style of architecture. Back of these buildings, is the
old town, on the hillside, with one street rising above
another, which gives the city a romantic appearance.
The river divides the city about equally, and is crossed
by many beautiful stone bridges. The water of the
lake, is of remarkable clearness, and in the strong
current of the river, it has a light blue color, reminding
one of water discharged from an indigo pot. There are
many mills and factories, on the banks of the river,
where the machinery is moved by the current; also
many wash houses, where women are seen washing at
all hours of the day, the rapid current of the river being
used as a washtub.

Geneva has many factories, where watches, jewelry,
and musical instruments are made, and from this source
the city has acquired most of her wealth. The watches
made here, are mostly of a good quality, and a high
price. The low priced, and worthless watches, marked
Geneva, are principally made in the adjoining towns.

From Geneva, emanated some of the religious, and
political doctrines, which now govern a large portion of
the world. Here lived and died, John Calvin, whose
mighty eloquence shook Catholicism to the center, and
from whose teachings, much of Europe derived their
form of faith, and which were transported by our pilgrim
fathers, to the shores of New England. Here too lived
Rousseau, the most accomplished of all infidel writers,
and here in Geneva, his colossal statue adorns the public

parks, and the monument to his memory is the admiration of all beholders. But Calvin's grave is neglected and the place where he was buried, forgotten. History says that he was buried in the cemetery of Plain Palais. While walking through the grounds of this cemetery, I inquired for Calvin's grave, but no one could tell me where it was. The sexton took me to one corner of the grounds, and pointed out a small square stone, rising about four inches above ground, with J. C. on it, saying here he was buried; but this spot is not generally conceded to be his burial place; tradition points to another part of these grounds.

In the old part of the city, stands St. Peter's Church, which still contains the same pulpit, from which Calvin preached, and by the side of the pulpit, is the chair of state, where he sat in judgement, over the temporal affairs of Geneva. While sitting in this chair, Calvin ordered Dr. Servetus to be burnt at a stake, outside of the city walls, because he would not subscribe to the orthodox faith. A short distance from St. Peter's Church, is the house where Calvin lived and died.

In the cemetery of Plain Palais, I saw the tombs of Sir Humphrey Davy, Sir Charles Napier, as well as many English authors and statesmen, who came here for the restoration of health, and here left their remains.

LAKE GENEVA AND SURROUNDINGS.

Lake Geneva is the largest of all the lakes in Switzerland, being fifty-five miles long, and six miles across at

the widest place. This lake has considerable commerce;
besides several lines of steamboats, there are sail vessels
running to different ports along its shores. Unlike
many of the Swiss lakes, where the scenery is wild,
with rocky cliffs rising high above the water, and
covered with perpetual snow, here the land rises
gradually from the waters edge, and its slopes are
covered with vineyards, farm and pasture lands, among
which are many fine old towns and cities.

Leaving Geneva in the morning, aboard of a fine
little steamer, we had a delightful sail up the lake,
giving us a good chance to view the beautiful scenery
along its shores. Above Geneva, on high land, overlooking the lake, is the house where Lord Byron lived
for many years, and where he wrote many of his poems.
Farther up the lake, is the chateau of Madam de Stael,
and also the one formerly occupied by different members
of the Bonaparte family. Near the head of the lake we
came to the Castle of Chillon, which has been immortalized by a poem of Byron. This castle is built on an
isolated rock out in the lake, and is connected with the
shore by a wooden bridge. History says, this castle
was built in the eleventh century, and became famous
under the rule of Peter of Savoy, who used it as a
prison, where many of the early church reformers were
confined. The castle is now used as a magazine, for
military stores, but a part of it remains the same as it
was in former times. Visitors are conducted through
it, and things of interest pointed out. Byron in his
Prisoner of Chillon, describes the suffering captive,

chained to a rock for six long years, in an ill-ventilated basement, which was only lighted by the reflection of the sun from the waters of the lake. This place was pointed out to us, and the ring in the stone pillar, to which the prisoner was chained, is still hanging, and the stone floor around it, is much worn by his pacing back and forth. On this pillar, Byron cut his name, and many others have followed his example. In one part of the castle, is a beam, black with age, where the condemned were hung, and in another place there is a small dark stairway of three steps; the victim found no fourth step, but was precipitated eighty feet down into the lake below.

ST. MAURICE.

Twelve miles above the head of lake Geneva, and in the valley of the Rhone, is located the old city of St. Maurice. This city is wedged in between the river and mountain, with houses built of gray stone, all clustered together, having narrow streets, and dirty alleys. On the west side of it is a cliff of rocks, rising almost per-.pendicularly, one thousand feet in hight, and houses are built against it, forming one side of their walls. On this rock, four hundred feet above the street, is a recess, cut out of the cliff, and in it, is a chapel, which was built over eight hundred years ago, and close by it, is a small house in the rock, where a monk lives, to take care of the chapel. This monk, is now eighty-five years old, living a life of a hermit, and has not been down from the rock, for fifty-three years. When he dies, another monk who is elected from those of the order of St. Maurice takes his place. The chapel is reached by a long flight of winding steps, cut out of the rock, and guarded by an iron railing. Morning and evening, people are seen climbing up these steps, to attend worship in the chapel.

Near the center of the city stands the old abbey of St. Maurice, built according to history in the year 365, by order of Constantine the Great, and at the time Christianity was first introduced among the Alps. On this abbey, are fourteen chime bells, which can be heard for miles away, and the sound re-echoes from the mountains, appearing like a band of music. From the sound of these bells, originated the idea of bell music, which has filled the world with Swiss bell ringers.

CHAPTER IX.

GORGE OF TRIENT.

In the valley of the Rhone a few miles above St. Maurice, is the Gorge of Trient, which is thought by many to be the greatest curiosity in Switzerland. It consists of a singular rent in the mountain, through which the river Trient passes, to enter the valley of the Rhone. After paying one franc each, for a ticket, we were conducted through this gorge, and beheld the wonderful works of nature. Here is a narrow passage, with rocks rising perpendicularly on either side, one thousand feet in hight, forming a wild looking chasm, where the sun never shines. Scaffolding of plank, nearly one half mile in length, is suspended by irons, put into the rock above, so that people can pass up to the head of the gorge with perfect safety. Along this narrow foot-bridge, we followed our guide, turning this way, then that, under leaning rocks, crossing and re-crossing the gorge, while thirty feet below us, runs the river, high from the melting of snow, roaring, and foaming,

P

as it pitches headlong over rocks. At the head of this gorge, is a cascade, where the river is confined to a narrow passage, and falls fifty feet. Below us, was the foaming water, fresh from the glaciers, sending up cold spray, and on either side of us, was the winding, and zigzag formation of the over-hanging rocks, while one thousand feet above us, was a narrow rent in the rocks, through which the light of day penetrated, making it the wildest, and grandest scenery I ever beheld.

Some distance below the Gorge of Trient, are the falls of Sallenche, one hundred and twenty feet high. Near these falls, is an opening in the mountain, caused by a landslide, which has filled up the valley to a considerable hight. This is said to have occurred over one thousand years ago, destroying the city of Epaunum, which stood in the valley below. A similar landslide, consisting of a torrent of mud and rock, descended from this mountain in 1835, cutting a passage through the forest, snapping off trees as twigs, destroying houses and farms, and covering the valley for some ways. The country along this part of the valley, looks desolate; farms are filled up with large rocks, and many houses are abandoned.

MARTIGNY.

Is an old Swiss town, situated in the valley of the Rhone, and contains but few attractions for strangers. On the side of the mountain overlooking the town, is to be seen the ruin of an old castle, which was built in

THE HOSPICE OF ST. BERNARD

the twelfth century, and at one time was the home of Peter of Savoy, from which that tyrant issued laws to govern the surrounding country. Here in Martigny, is a convent of the order of St. Augustine, where the monks of St. Bernard have their head quarters, and from which the guards on the mountain are relieved at intervals. The climate here is subject to great changes, one day warm, and the next cold and damp, caused by the wind blowing off the snowy mountains. Many of the people are afflicted with the goitre, (an enlargement of the neck). I have noticed this disease in other parts of Switzerland, but no place so much as here; nearly one half the women we meet have this complaint. It was at Martigny, that Bonaparte collected his grand army for crossing the Alps, and many things relating to that event, are related by old citizens of the place.

Fourteen miles south of Martigny, is the great St. Bernard Pass, which is the oldest, and most noted of all the passes of the Alps. Here is a hospice kept by monks, and large enough to accommodate one hundred and fifty persons. Travelers are entertained here free of charge, but are always expected to put into the contribution box money equal to a hotel bill. Near the hospice is the Morgue, or charnel house, where are deposited, and in a good state of preservation, a large number of dead bodies, being the remains of persons who lost their lives by snow storms or avalanches, while crossing the mountains.

FORCLOZ PASS.

At Martigny we left our baggage in exchange for alpine staffs, and commenced a tour over the mountains on foot; taking the Tete Noire road for Chamouni, a distance of twenty-two miles, most of the way over stones and rocks, along a crooked mule path, and up and down steep mountains. For the first few miles up the mountain, the ascent was easy, being through a chestnut forest, among which were apple and pear trees, with here and there small farms and dwellings occupied by mountaineers. After some hours of hard walking, we reached the summit at Forcloz Pass, where there is a hotel and custom house, it being on the dividing line between Switzerland and Savoy. The whole military force at this point guarding the Swiss frontier, consists of an old soldier, with a rusty fowling piece, and living in an eight by ten shanty called the custom house. This officer feels the importance of his position, acting both in a civil and military capacity. With a big feather in his cap, and a gun on his shoulder, he stops all people with valises demanding one franc for examining it. Some of our party refused to pay him fees, when he told them to go on as he could not afford to examine baggage for nothing.

We remained all night at the Forcloz Pass, and experienced some of the peculiarities of mountain atmosphere. Although it was August, the night was cold and damp, and a feather bed, used in this country for covering, was not out of place. Next morning a cloud had settled on the mountain, which was black and thick, wetting a person when out of doors.

The road from Forcloz Pass to Chamouni, presents some of the wildest scenery met with among the mountains. Sometimes by the side of a frightful precipice guarded only by a pole, then under leaning rocks and tunnels cut through the cliff, then by the side of roaring water with here and there a cascade. Along this road are many shrines containing images of the Virgin Mary, crucifixion of Christ etc., also crosses and monuments erected to the memory of persons who lost their lives here by avalanches. On the road we met large companies of travelers, some on foot, others on mules, while a few were carried by two men in a chair, also men carrying baggage on their backs, and mules loaded with trunks.

CHAMOUNI.

The village of Chamouni is located at the foot of Mt. Blanc, and in the valley of Chamouni. This valley is said to be two thousand feet higher than that of the Rhone, and surrounded as it is by snow and ice, causes vegetation to be more backward than in other valleys among the Alps. One mile above the village of Chamouni is the Mer de Glass, (which means sea of ice), extending down into the valley, and from which comes forth a large stream of water, roaring and foaming as it pitches over rocks on its way to the lake. For three hours we plodded our way up the mountain by the side of the Mer de Glass, over stones, between rocks, and along frightful cliffs with steps in one place cut into the rocks, and guarded only by a wire. Below us, was this sea of ice, with crags of it standing up 'in wild masses like pyramids, between which are cracks in the ice ten or twelve feet wide, where no bottom can be seen. Before reaching the top, some of our party showed symptoms of giving out, but our guide, who was a Swiss maiden, (to whom we gave the name of Chamois, on account of her sprightliness in jumping from rock to rock), gave encouragement to them, by saying: in a few minutes more the summit would be reached. At last we came to the head of the path, where we left the rocks, and took to the ice, crossing the Mer de Glass we descended the mountain on the opposite side, and arrived safe in town, but much fatigued after our long tramp.

While we were at Chamouni, a party of tourists ascended Mt. Blanc, which caused much excitement among the people. The ascent of this mountain is of rare occurrence, and if successful, it is regarded a great exploit, as many undertaking it, lose their lives in the attempt. Guides charge one hundred dollars to conduct a party up the mountain, and it requires three days to make an ascension, which can only be accomplished by those accustomed to climbing mountains, or that have brought themselves into training for that purpose. The first night is spent in a cave of rocks, high up among the ice crags, and the next day the summit is reached when the party returns to the cave to spend the second night.

The day was clear and bright, and crowds of people with their glasses ascended the opposite mountain to watch the tourists. At four o'clock in the morning they left the cave, and at half past twelve, they reached the summit which was announced at the village by firing six salutes with a cannon. At six o'clock in the evening again the firing of cannon gave notice of their safe arrival at the cave. I have talked with different persons who have ascended Mt. Blanc, and they say the cold is severe, and the air so rarefied that it is difficult to breath; on making great exertions, blood would gush from the nose and mouth.

Some miles up the mountain, between the Mer de Glass and Mt. Blanc is a fertile slope where grass grows, and flowers bloom, while surrounded on all sides by snow and ice. To this place, the people of the valley drive their cattle each summer to feed on the grass. A road is prepared for their transit, by cutting the ice with axes, so as to prevent the cattle from falling into crevices. All things being ready, the cattle are dirven up the mountain and across the ice, attended by men, women and children, besides lookers on to see the sport. One man remains with the cattle, as herdsman who carries with him a supply of bread and cheese, while a cow supplies him with milk. For months he remains here, guarding the herd, sleeping in a cave, eating his bread and cheese, and meditating upon the wonders of nature.

COL DE BALME.

From the valley of Chamouni, we ascended the Col
de Balme, by a stony mule path which runs zigzag up
the mountain, so as to keep the grade about equal.
This mountain contains neither trees nor shrubs, but a
species of wire grass grows on it, and cattle, sheep and
goats, are herded here. For four hours we continued
our way up the mountain, sometimes resting by springs
of cold water, then again stopping to eat a species of
huckleberry, which grows on the rocks. On the summit
are two hotels consisting of temporary buildings, and
occupied only during the summer season. Although it
was a bright August day we found the weather at this
high altitude quite cold, and the hotel was without
fire, except in the cook stove, and the fuel used
consisted of cattle chips, which gave a very offensive
smell.

The view from the summit of the Col de Balme, is
very grand, and is probably not equalled by any other
scenery among the Alps. Sixty miles to the north-east
we could see the Barnese chain of mountains, spread
out before us like a painted panorama, with the snow-
capped Jungfrau in its midst. South of us, in plain
view were two peaks, between which is the great St.
Bernard Pass. Near by us, were those bold rocky crags
which form such an important feature in the Alpine
chain, while before us was the great monarch of the
Alps, Mt. Blanc, nearly three miles high, being the

highest point in Europe. At the foot of this mountain the view is not good, notwithstanding it can be seen from bottom to top; much of its beauty is lost by the obstruction of other peaks. But from here almost every gorge, cliff of rocks, and even the cracks in the ice are visible, and for many miles below its summit shows a smooth surface rising like a sugar loaf, and of chalky whiteness.

After four days climbing up and down mountains, over stone and rocks, snow and ice, making the whole distance traveled on foot, more than one hundred miles, we returned to Martigny, none the worse for wear, except in shoe leather.

SIMPLON PASS.

From Martigny we ascended the valley of the Rhone as far as Sion. This is an old Swiss town with a few thousand inhabitants having narrow streets and high stone houses which are built in a cluster together. Here are three old castles, two of which are now in ruins, together with the bishop's palace, and many old churches which date back to the eleventh century, giving the town a feudal aspect, while it looks as though it might have seen better days. At Sion the railroad ends, and the only conveyance eastward is by diligence, which is both slow and expensive, and but little improvement on the old fashioned way of staging in the United States. These diligences are built high and long, with three compartments, seating in all eight persons, and drawn

Q

by five horses, which are changed every six miles on the road.

Here is the commencement of the great Simplon Pass, the high-road across the Alps into Italy, distant one hundred and twenty miles. For thirty miles the road follows up the valley of the Rhone, then diverging, it takes to the mountains. On this road we passed through the town of Visp, which became noted in 1855, on account of its being visited by many shocks of earthquakes, which continued for weeks, throwing down many buildings and cracking others, while the inhabitants left their homes and camped in the valley. When we visited this place it was suffering from a calamity namely: floods of water. The channel of the Rhone here is higher than the valley, being guarded by a stone wall, and the present great freshet having made a breach in this wall, destroying the crops, and washing away many houses while the water was still running knee deep through the streets of the town. The inhabitants, including women and children, were engaged in repairing the walls, so as to turn the water away from their homes; while the town and country around it looked desolate. If I lived here I should certainly leave, and seek a home on the prairies of the west.

Some miles above Visp, is the old village of Glys, a place distinguished by its old Byzantine Church, said to have been built one thousand years ago. And by the side of it is the charnel house, containing more than ten thousand skulls, as well as skeletons of saints, who lived at the time christianity was first introduced among the Alps.

At Brieg, the road leaves the valley of the Rhone, and for sixteen miles it has a gradual ascent up the mountain, turning and winding about in various directions, so as to keep the grade equal; sometimes by the side of high precipices where the road has been cut out of a cliff of rocks, then across viaducts, over frightful gorges, and through dark tunnels and arched galleries, making it without doubt the greatest work of the kind in the world.

This road was built by Napoleon for the purpose of transporting his army back and forth from France to Italy, and to avoid the difficulty again occurring which he experienced in crossing the Alps at the great St. Bernard's Pass. The road is very wide, well macadamized and contains ten tunnels, over six hundred bridges, with many galleries, and along it are twenty houses of refuge to lodge travelers, as well as laborers employed in repairing and taking care of the road. Before reaching the summit we came to a very dangerous part of the road, where avalanches had carried away the guards and left the highway exposed. Here are many long galleries through which the road passes, being built to protect it from avalanches. These galleries are constructed of thick stone walls, arched over at the top, and lighted by openings in the walls at long intervals. At one place there is a large stream of water running from the glaciers above, passing over the road, and making a nice waterfall.

At last the summit was reached, being far above the line of vegetation, and in the vicinity of snow and ice, while below us in plain view, and almost under us, lies the Rhone valley, with the city of Brieg, which we had left six hours before. Here on the summit of the mountain is a hospice, similar to the one at St. Bernard, which is a place of stopping for all travelers crossing the mountain. This place is kept by monks of the order of St. Augustine, who are very polite to strangers, showing them through the building, and offering them such eatables as the establishment affords. They offered us bread and cheese to eat, with cider and wine to drink. Politeness required us to partake of it whether hungry or not. There are many dogs of the St. Bernard breed kept here, to assist in finding travelers who may be caught in a snow storm, which frequently occurs during the winter months. Whoever visits this pass, of whatever country, or religion he may be, will always find a friendly greeting, both from monks and dogs.

From here we commenced a descent of the mountain, and for fifteen miles the grade of the road is about the same as the ascent. With rubbers on the coach wheels and the horses in a fast trot, with their bells ringing, and with the constant cracking of the drivers whip, brought us down the mountain in half the time occupied in ascending it. The southern slope of the mountain is more interesting than the northern, and is said to present the finest scenery met with among the Alps. The gorge of Gondo, is both grand and wild, with overhanging rocks above, and frightful precipices below, where the rocks rise like walls on either side, showing only a narrow strip of sky above. The roaring of the water as it pitches madly over the rocks, with the rattling of the diligence as it passes across iron viaducts to enter a tunnel through the cliffs, and again comes out of the dark cavern of the rocks to be wet by the spray of the cascades below, form a picture probably not met with in any other part of the world.

While enjoying the beautiful scenery on the road, the Italian frontier is crossed, and we find ourselves in a different climate, where chestnut and other forest trees grow. Instead of barren rocks with snow and ice, we saw fields of grain and grass, with orchards and vineyards loaded with fruit. Here are villages built of white stone, with old churches containing tall square bell towers, and narrow crooked streets, full of organ grinders. And here were lazy lazzaroni, clothed in greasy roundabouts with red knit caps as well as burly priests dressed in uniform, showing the country to be Italian in every respect.

At Isella, a small town on the Italian frontier, we stopped at the custom house, where our baggage underwent an examination. As soon as the stages stopped they were surrounded by a large number of women who would assist in handling baggage and looking after the interest of strangers, so they would not be imposed upon by the custom house officer. We could not understand what these women said to us, but supposed it to be kind words, for it brought roars of laughter from the bystanders.

We passed on this road a number of marble quarries, with large boulders of the same which had rolled down from the mountain, and lying around loose. For forty miles the telegraph poles are marble, being composed of one solid piece about fifteen feet long; and many of the farm and village houses are also constructed of marble.

At Stresa, we boarded a steamer and had a sail on the beautiful lake of Maggiore. This lake is forty miles long, and from three to seven wide. While steaming down the lake we had a fine view of Mt. Rosa, one of the most celebrated peaks of the Alps. Although more than fifty miles away, it appeared close by, and its snow-capped summit looked like a white cloud high up in the zenith. From the south end of the lake we took the cars for Milan, forty miles distant.

CHAPTER X.

The city of Milan, the former capital of Lombardy contains 212,000 inhabitants, and stands on a level plain. It is well built, having many wide and smoothly flagged streets, houses high, many of which are coated with marble, and the general appearance of the city is attractive. The great cathedral of Milan is said to be the most elegant structure in the world, and attracts universal admiration. It is constructed of white marble of a gothic style of architecture, and contains one hundred and thirty-five spires. On the top of each of these spires stands a colossal marble statue. The center one is three hundred and thirty-six feet high, and capped by a gilt statue. The outside walls are ornamented with nineteen hundred and twenty-three marble statues, and the inside walls have six hundred and seventy-nine statues. This church was commenced over five hundred years ago, and is not yet completed, as additional statuary is placed on its walls every year.

In the basement, under the high altar, is the Virgin's chapel containing many things of great antiquity, such as the massive gold and silver ware used in sacramental service by Constantine the Great. Also many relics said to have been brought from Jerusalem by Empress Helena. Among which are three nails from the cross, the shrowd of the Virgin Mary, and seamless coat of Christ.

Here in Milan is the greatest arcade in the world, built at the crossing of two wide streets, which takes in four squares, with a high dome in the center. In this dome are gas burners a short distance apart, and to light them a fire car is put in motion, which performs the whole circle lighting each burner as it passes. The floor of this mammoth arcade is composed of marble (mosaic work), inlaid with various colors, and representing different kinds of flowers, Italian coat of arms etc.

Many of the hotels in Milan have an open court in the center which connects with the street by a wide door, so that carriages having guests for the hotel can drive in to unload. All of the first class hotels here, have marble floors and stairs throughout the whole building.

PLAINS OF LOMBARDY.

The plains of Lombardy extend from the southern slope of the Alps, to the head of the Adriatic Sea, a distance of several hundred miles. These plains have long been the bone of contention between Italy and

Austria, as well as the scene of many hard fought battles. Here the country is level, without timber or fencing, and is under a high state of cultivation, producing various kinds of grain and fruits. Silks, wine, and maccaroni, constitute its principal exports. Mulberry trees for the silk culture are planted in rows all over the country, and on these are trained the grape vine, instead of on short poles as in other countries. In France and Germany, there are large vineyards, but here on the plains of Lombardy, the whole country is one vast vineyard. In traveling a hundred miles or more, we were all the while in the midst of it.

In traveling several hundred miles through the plains of Lombardy, we visited a number of old cities, much celebrated in ancient history, as well as a number of battle fields memorable for the past. Forty miles north of Milan we came to Lake Como, celebrated in all ages on account of its mild climate and beautiful scenery. This lake is thirty-five miles long and from two to three miles wide, and on it are running two lines of steamboats. Much has been written by travelers about the beauty and enchanting scenery of this lake. But these glowing accounts must have been written by persons who have never seen the lakes of Switzerland, which far surpass it in every particular. In the surroundings of Lake Como there are neither fine forests, rugged rocks, nor snow-capped peaks; but a barren elevation too large for hills, and too small for mountains.

At the south end of the lake, and wedged in between two hills, is located the old city of Como, where Pliny lived

R

nearly two thousand years ago, and also where Volta
lived and died; a fine monumental statue of him stands
on the market square. Here in Como, as well as other
cities of northern Italy, the larger portion of the women
wear no shoes, but have a block of wood fastened on
the bottom of their feet by a strap around their instep.
Some of them wear stockings, while others have this
block of wood strapped on their bare feet. These blocks
make a terrible clattering on the sidewalk.

One hundred and twenty miles south-east of Como,
we came to Verona, a large city partly built of marble,
and at a distance looking like a city of palaces, with its
white houses and beautiful church domes. Here is the
ruin of an amphitheatre, built over two thousand years
ago, the walls of which are composed of marble and are
in a good state of preservation. Fronting the cathedral,
stands the colossal statue of Roland, and near it is that
of Oliver. In other parts of the city are many statues
and monuments erected to the memory of statesmen and
warriors of ancient Rome.

Near Lake Garda we saw the battle field of Solferino,
memorable for the war of 1859. The number of combatants engaged, and the many thousands slain, makes
this the greatest battle ever fought in Europe. This
battle field is a level plain extending from the lake to
the village of Solferino, and the whole of it can be seen
at one view. The different positions of the contending
armies were pointed out and explained to us by one
who was present at the time, and participated in the
battle. The buildings here, still show marks of this

dreadful conflict, and on different parts of the battle field are long rows of graves, surmounted with a cross and containing hundreds of slain.

Almost every town along the Austrian frontier is strongly fortified, and is memorable for bloody battles fought around their walls.

VENICE.

The city of Venice (styled the Queen of the Adriatic), stands off in the sea, three miles from the main land, and is connected with it only by a railroad bridge, all other communication with the shore is by boat. On approaching the city it was discovered that we were traveling on water, and people looking out of the car windows, would fall back in their seats with a shudder, as the thought of going to sea in a railroad train was not very agreeable. When we reached the city the large crowd of people passed through the depot into an open square where gondolas were in waiting to convey them to different parts of the city. There are many omnibus gondolas here which connect with the trains, and will seat twenty or thirty persons. These have cushioned seats, curtained windows, and are rowed by four men. For nearly two miles we glided on the way to our hotel, no rattling of carriages on the pavement, nor cracking of the driver's whips, nor swearing of dray-men, but quietly and smoothly we passed on to our place of destination. On our way we met a funeral procession consisting of some thirty gondolas draped in mourning, and with muffled oars. Farther on we met a large procession consisting of one hundred or more gondolas with a band of music, flags waving, and with loud cheering as they passed, celebrating some national event.

On our arrival in Venice we ascended the tower of St. Mark's, which is three hundred and sixteen feet high, the top of which is reached by an inclined plain of thirty-nine turnings. From this tower the whole city with its surroundings can be seen, as well as the Adriatic Sea for many miles, whitened with sails. Nothing can be more picturesque than a view from this tower, showing a large city with its many fine churches, palaces and piazzas far out at sea, with the blue waters of the Adriatic on every side. And here can be seen thousands of Gondolas running hither and thither through its numerous streets.

Where the city now stands were originally seventy-two small islands, and the foundation for the buildings was made by driving down piles into the marsh. The houses are mostly built of stone, five or six stories high, many of which are coated with marble or stucco, and show much architectural skill in their construction. The Church of St. Mark's, and the Palace of Doge, are among the finest buildings in the city. Adjoining these edifices is the great piazza of St. Mark, surrounded by fine buildings and flagged with smooth stone. For many centuries this square has been the head quarters of Venice. It was here Othello addressed the assembled senate, and here, Anthony stood when he appealed to the Roman soldiers to correct the evils of their rulers.

The grand canal, which is the Broadway of Venice, runs the whole length of the city, dividing it about equally, being winding, in the shape of an S, and is about three hundred feet in width. Along this canal are the principal hotels, stores and shipping houses, as well as the residences of the aristocracy of the city. There are no sidewalks along it, nor any of the streets of Venice, and the buildings rise straight up from the water's edge. All the principal streets of the city are canals, many of which are quite narrow, with buildings rising high above the water, giving them a dark and gloomy appearance. Most of the houses have both a water and a land entrance, the latter connects with a narrow alley a few feet in width, which is dark and gloomy. But here in these narrow passages are stores and shops, where thousands of people live and die, without ever having seen growing a stalk of corn, or a spire of wheat. Horses and carriages are never seen in Venice, as there is not a spot in the whole city where they could be used, and a horse or cow would be as great curiosity here, as an elephant or camel in the United States.

Among the great curiosities of Venice are the gondolas which are peculiar to this city, and I believe are not met with in any other part of the world. They are about thirty feet long, with their bow and stern rising some six feet above the water, and on the former is a large figure head made of polished steel. Many of these vessels are ornamented on the outside with carved work, painted black, and have cushioned seats, with a portable top letting down like that of a buggy. There are over four thousand of these gondolas in the city, in many of which the owner sleeps, and can be called at any time of night. At the hotels and all public places, they are in waiting for customers who wish to be carried to different parts of the city, and their charges are about the same as cabs in other cities. The gondolas are propelled by one oar, and the person using it stands up in the stern of the vessel running it through the narrow streets of the city with great rapidity.

According to history, Venice at one time was the greatest commercial city in the world; then its sails whitened every sea, and its ships were seen in every port. But of late it has lost much of its commerce, even the trade of the Adriatic mostly goes to Triest eighty miles east of it. Notwithstanding her fine churches, palaces and queenly appearance, she is a doomed city, unless some change is made in her commercial affairs.

The present population of Venice is one hundred and thirty thousand, and it has a free port.

CHAPTER XI.

Midway between the Mediteranean and Adriatic Seas, stands the old and much celebrated city of Bologna. Containing over one hundred thousand inhabitants, and surrounded by a high wall, through which are twelve gates guarded by soldiers who collect duties on produce going into the city. The aspect of the city is ancient and gloomy with narrow crooked streets, along which are arcades covering the sidewalk, causing the stores and shops along them to be dark and unattractive. Here in Bologna are two leaning towers, the highest of which is three hundred and twenty-one feet, and the date on its base shows that it was built in the year 1109.

A person traveling through Italy will be surprised at the magnitude of its churches, some of which cost millions of dollars, and occupied centuries in their construction. Small towns in some cases, contain churches more costly than any found in the United States. These churches were built by the government, and every person, rich or poor, contributed a part to their construction. And well may it be said that Italy is a country of rich churches, but poor people.

After remaining one day in Bologna, we took the cars for the west, passing up a valley where the hills were high on either side, until the hight of the Appennines was reached and crossed. The railroad across these mountains is considered the best specimen of engineering in Europe. In places it passes under cliffs of rocks, into tunnels, across frightful gorges spanned by iron viaducts, then zigzag along the mountain, being more of the time under ground than on top of it. At last the summit is reached, and the descent was made in the same way as the ascent. On reaching the valley below, a tower was pointed out marking the place where Cataline was defeated (B. C. 60), and beyond this tower we came to Pistiga. This is a manufacturing city, containing about twelve thousand inhabitants, and it is said that pistols were first made here, and from that circumstance derived their name.

LORETO.

On the eastern slope of the Appennines is located the celebrated town of Loreto, containing the sacred house or Santa Casa, which originally stood in Nazareth. According to tradition this wonderful house was the birthplace of Virgin Mary, and the scene of annunciation as well as the residence of the holy family after their return from Egypt. In the year 1294, it was transported by divine agency from Palestine to Italy, and after various attempts to land somewhere in the Pope's dominions, it finally settled down at Loreto where it still remains. A number of persons who lived in that day, and whose names are recorded in the church book, certify that they saw this house floating through the air, sometimes over the Adriatic Sea, then over the mountains and plains, but was guided by the angel Gabriel to its final resting place. This miraculous story is not only believed by the ignorant and superstitious people here, but the intelligent and educated regard it a miracle which they dare not question. Even popes and crowned heads, have worshiped at its shrine, and for more than five hundred years pilgrims from all parts of Europe have visited it.

This sacred house is about twenty-five feet long, and fifteen feet wide, constructed with brick, and enclosed in a marble case, which stands in one wing of a church. It has an ancient appearance, with only one window, and one door; its floor consists of red and white marble, the original one having been lost in its miraculous flight from Palestine. In one part of this house is a shrine containing among other things, the statue of the Virgin and Infant Christ, said to have been cut by St. Luke out of the cedar of Lebanon. Around this shrine are a large number of silver lamps, which are kept continually burning, and before it at all hours of the day people can be seen kneeling in prayer.

s

FLORENCE.

The city of Florence has frequently been styled the Athens of Europe, and the cradle of fine arts, from which has emanated statues and paintings, that now adorn the museums and palaces throughout the whole civilized world. Here are collected the best sculptors and painters of all countries, among whom are some from the United States, who have already acquired fame and distinction, and bid fair to eclipse those of the old world.

Florence is built on a level plain, on both sides of the river Arno, over which are seven bridges. The city contains a population of one hundred and fifty thousand, and is surrounded by a high wall, through which are seven gates guarded by soldiers who collect duties on almost every article brought into the city. Most of the streets are narrow, but the main thoroughfares are of good width, flagged with square blocks of stone which makes them smooth and attractive. The buildings are high, composed of stone, and show much beauty in their construction. In different parts of the city are public squares called piazzas, which are paved with flag stones, but contain neither trees, grass nor flowers. Public squares of this kind are common in all the cities of Italy. Many of the streets and small squares are filled up with market stalls, making it almost impossible to pass through them during business hours.

The public puildings of Florence constitute its most

FLORENCE FROM THE SOUTHEAST.

striking feature, many of which for elegance and beauty surpass those of other Italian cities, while the squares adjoining them are filled with statues which represent warriors, and statesmen of past ages. The Duomo, or great cathedral of Florence, is the largest and most conspicuous building in the city, and its lofty dome towers up above all other objects, constituting a land mark to guide a stranger in his walks. This cathedral was commenced in the year 1298, and is still in an unfinished condition; workmen are still employed on it. The outside is coated with marble of white, black, and green colors, intermixed so as to make the prospective views beautiful in the extreme. The inside of the cathedral is coated with marble and gilt. The dome is three hundred and seventy-eight feet high; on the inside are paintings representing paradise on one side, and punishment of the condemned on the other. By the side of this cathedral stands its great bell tower, two hundred and seventy-six feet high, constructed of colored marble, and it is said to be the most elegant tower in Europe. The accompaning view of Florence shows this cathedral on the right, while on the left, is seen one of the beautiful bridges across the Arno.

On the piazza of St. Marco, is situated the great Florentine factory of mosaic work, belonging to the government. Here are manufactured articles of furniture which sell as high as an half million dollars each.

The Uffizi museum, next to the Louvre of Paris, is the largest in Europe, consisting of many halls and galleries where everything is arranged according to its order,

and to examine them would require many days. Here
are the life size busts, cut in marble, and said to be
taken from life of all the Roman Emperors, as well as
many warriors and statesmen of their day. In one
room are many sarcophagi taken from the catacombs
of Vatterre, which contain the remains of people who
lived before the Christian era. On the covers of many
of these sarcophagi, is the likeness, cut in stone, of the
person entombed therein, some of which are in a sitting,
while others are in a lying position. From Uffizi museum, there is a gallery connecting it with Pitti Palace
on the opposite side of the river. This gallery is about
one fourth of a mile in length, passing through blocks
of buildings, across streets, and over the river on a
bridge. Along the whole length of this gallery the
walls are hung with paintings and tapestry. Pitti
Palace is the present residence of the king of Italy, but
twelve apartments of it belong to the Uffizi museum,
and are open to the public.

Close by Pitti Palace is located the museum of natural
history, with an astronomical observatory, and also a
large collection of instruments which were used by the
early teachers of science. And here is the temple of
Galileo, built to his memory, and containing with other
things the great telescope with which he discovered the
satellites of Jupiter. And here is Galileo's statue taken
from life, which shows him to have been a man of great
physical, as well as mental powers. I visited the
studios of Powers, Hart, and Simmons, and other
American sculptors, all of whom I found busy at work,

gathering the laurels from the brows of sculptors of the old world.

Much has been said about the beautiful situation of Florence, its mild and healthful climate, its smooth flagged streets, its fine edifices, and its artistic treasures. All of these combined make Florence the most attractive place in Europe, and it was with feelings of regret, that I left it, for the city of the popes. But everything comes to'an end, and so did my stay in Florence.

RUINS OF FIESOLE.

Three miles from Florence, on a high hill, one thousand feet above the plains of Arno, is to be seen the ruins of Fiesole, which have been so often referred to in the history of ancient Rome. The road leading to these ruins, passes across the plain, by the side of beautiful villas which are surrounded by parks, and flower gardens, where fountains of water are spouting forth among the orange and lemon trees. Some of these villas have been the residences of distinguished men of past ages, one of which is called Arcetri Villa, where Galileo lived and died, and where he made many of his observations in astronomy. Here he rambled over these beautiful grounds after he had lost his eye sight, and here Milton visited him, and wrote that celebrated poem describing this villa.

Fiesole was one of the oldest cities of Italy, and a place of great importance during the time of the Roman Republic. It was here Cataline retreated after his defeat

(B. C. 60), and surrounded as he was by the strong walls of the city, bid defiance to the Roman authorities. Some of his treasure, consisting of the coin of that day, and buried here at the time, was found about forty years ago. Part of the city wall is still standing, with two of its ruined gates, also the remains of a great amphitheatre, together with some of its ruined temples and palaces.

Modern Fiesole is but a small village, occupying a portion of the ground within the walls of the ruined city. A monastery occupies the site of the old fortification, and a view from the terrace of its walls is very fine. Here can be seen high hills without forest trees, but covered with orchards of olive and fig, between which are vineyards, and cultivated fields. While below us is a large plain with its many towns and villages, and through which runs the river Arno, winding back and forth like a serpent. Right before us, and looking like a painted panorama, lies the beautiful city of Florence, with its fine churches and palaces, while far distant can be seen the blue outlines of the Appennine mountanins.

After spending the day among the ruins of this Etruscan city, and meditating upon the many great events that took place here thousands of years ago, the actors of which are now sleeping in the catacombs close by, we returned to Florence much delighted with our visit to the ruins of Fiesole.

On the morning of the first of October we were on the cars for Rome which is two hundred and thirty miles distant. The railroad between these points follows the western slope of the Appennines, and the country is hilly, without timber, and is in a bad state of cultivation, differing very much from the northern part of Italy. We passed on our way, many old towns and cities which are built on high hills surrounded with walls and high watch towers, giving them a feudal aspect.

On passing the Italian frontier, the Pope's officers came aboard of the cars demanding passports which they keep, until our arrival at Rome. All that were not provived with passports were stopped, and sent back on the next train.

CHAPTER XII.

ROME.

The present population of Rome is about two hundred thousand. The city lies on both sides of the river Tiber, fourteen miles from its mouth. It is surrounded by a wall thirteen miles in length, fifty feet high, ornamented with three hundred towers, and pierced by twenty-one gates. Ancient Rome was built on seven hills, three of which are covered by the modern city, and the other four contain the ruins of the old, all of which lie within the city walls. The churches, of which there are three hundred and sixty-four, form the most conspicuous feature of the city. Most of these churches are coated both outside and in, with colored marble, and contain fine paintings and statuary. Many of them have been built of material taken from temples and palaces of ancient Rome, and a few of the old heathen temples have been changed into the form of christian worship.

The streets of Rome are narrow and winding, paved

with small flat stone, without sidewalks, and are dirty
and filthy, producing a great variety of offensive smells.
The Corso extending from Capitoline Hill to the gate of
Del Popolo, is the great thoroughfare of the city.
Along it are many fine piazzas and palaces, as well as
the best stores of the city.

The river Tiber running through the city is a small
dirty looking stream, with but little commerce, and
crossed by many stone bridges. But small as this river
is, it once floated the Roman fleet, which conquered the
world. On the right bank of the river, stands the great
castle of Stanjelo, built in a circular form, and constituting one of the principal land marks of Rome.

In the north-west part of the city near St. Peter's
church, is located the Vatican, containing the great
Roman museum, as well as a royal palace, the present
residence of the Pope. To examine this museum, would
require a number of days, as the collection of ancient
paintings and sculptures is the largest in the world.
Here are to be seen manuscripts of the bible, which were
written in the second century, also the original
manuscript of the works of St. Jerome, written in the
year 364.

The catacombs of Rome are situated outside of the
city walls, and on account of their historical celebrity
and connection with primitive Christians, are frequently visited by travelers. The entrance to these
catacombs is through a church, and a monk with lighted
candles conducts the party through these vaulted chambers which are said to have been the burial place for more

T

than six million of human beings. In some places bones
and stacks of skulls are seen, and occasionally a sar-
cophagus containing the ashes of some distinguished
person. In these catacombs are large chambers where
the early christians met to worship, and here many of
them fled to escape persecution, living and dying in
these loathsome vaults. One of these large chambers,
called Saint's Chapel, is said to have been a place of
worship for converts under the preaching of Paul and
Peter, and on that account, is regarded by the monks
as the most sacred place in the catacombs. In this
apartment are many devices on the walls, cut into the
rock, and bearing date A. D. 92, representing Christian
ordinances, one of which shows baptism by pouring.

In the East part of the city is located the convent of
Holy Friars, which is occupied by some four hundred
monks of that order. This convent consists of a number
of large buildings, and in the back part of which are
eight rooms filled with the bones of more than fifty
thousand monks. These bones have been accumulating
for over one thousand years, and are put up according
to their order, with columns of skulls and shank bones,
rising ten feet high. On the walls and ceiling, bones
of various sizes are arranged with much skill, representing the Pope's coat of arms, different kinds of animals,
flowers, etc. Among these bones are many sainted
monks wrapped in metalic robes, and are well preserved
mummies. Some of these are lying on shelves among
stacks of skulls, others sitting or standing, and all have
on their breasts their name and time of death, some of

which date back to the eighth century. The ground floor of these rooms is fully occupied with graves of monks, and when one dies, the remains of another are taken up, and his bones placed on the shelves; thus, room is made in the burial ground for the new occupant.

In the old part of the city among the ruins of ancient Rome, is the church of St. John Laterena, which was built in the fourth century, and by order of Constantine the Great, consequently is the oldest church in Europe. In the chapel of this church are to be seen the holy stairs which were brought from Jerusalem by Empress Helena in the year 326, being the same upon which Christ ascended to the judgment seat of Pilate. These stairs are constructed of white marble, with twenty-eight steps, and are covered on the top with thick plank, to prevent wearing. No one is allowed to ascend these stairs except on his knees. At all hours of the day, people of various ages, with decrepit old men and women are seen going up and down these stairs on their knees.

On the southern slope of Capitoline Hill stands the celebrated Marmertine prison, which is said to be the oldest building now standing in Rome. This prison is memorable as the place of confinement of the leaders in Cataline's rebellion, (B. C. 60), as well as the place where St. Peter was imprisoned. The upper part of this prison is now used for a church, being dedicated to St. Peter, and on the day of our visit, was full of priests and monks who had come as pilgrims from different parts of Europe, to celebrate the anniversary of the Apostle's birth. A monk with a lighted lamp conducted

us down two flights of stairs, into a dark dungeon cut
out of a rock, and lighted only by a single lamp which
hung on the wall. The only means of ventilation to
this vault is by a small circular opening in the ceiling
which connects with the room above. Here, said the
monk, in this loathsome prison, St. Peter was confined,
and here is the stone pillar with the ring still in it where
he was chained, and here also is the water with which
he baptized the jailor. At the same time uncovering a
small tank of water, sunk below the level of the stone
floor, and dipping up some of it he handed us to drink.

There are many things here which the monk pointed
out as being connected with the imprisonment of St.
Peter. Some of which would require more credulity than
I possess, to believe. But there can be no doubt about
the Apostle being imprisoned here, as it was a matter
of too great importance to be overlooked by early
church historians, and it is also corroborated by Plu-
tarch who wrote in that day, and who was at that time
a resident of Rome.

Rome at one time was the mistress of the world,
counting its inhabitants by millions; then its power
and fame was acknowledged by all nations. But its
glory has departed, and it now only contains the relics
of its former grandeur. No longer the home of the
great orators and statesmen, but where poverty, ignorance and priestcraft reigns supreme, and is without
doubt the worst governed city in Europe. Martial law
is in force here, and no one is allowed to enter or leave
the city without a passport. The police are all secret,

some in citizen's dress, others in a garb of a priest or street sweeper. And these policemen make frequent arrests of persons for using seditious language. Here there is a system of religious intolerance, and all Protestants are compelled to hold their meetings outside of the city walls.

The Pope is frequently seen riding through the streets, always accompained by a troop of horsemen and carriages containing dignitaries of the church. No sovereign in Europe meets with such cordial reception from his subjects as he. With the Pope there is a religious awe which appears to fascinate all that look upon him. When his holiness is known to be coming through a street all the carriages turn out of it, and the people riding in them, get out and take off their hats.

The first day I spent in Rome, while riding through a street, I found it in great confusion, people running this way and that, crying Pope, Pope. I found my carriage up against a building, and the driver motioning me to get out, but I remained seated, feeling more safe in the carriage than in the crowd. To my surprise, I found the driver and two other men whom I supposed were policemen, helping me out. They motioned me to take off my hat, but I shook my head. Again with angry jestures they ordered my hat off, but my hat remained on my head notwithstanding their threats.

CHURCH OF ST. PETER.

This mammoth structure is located near the Tiber, in the north-west part of the city, and is said to occupy the spot where once stood Nero's circus, as well as the place where St. Peter was martyred. This building with its chapels, porticos and piazzas covers eight acres of ground, and occupied one hundred and seventy-six years in its construction, at a cost of fifty million dollars. The front of the church is ornamented with marble columns ninety-two feet high, between which are iron gates that open into a vestibule four hundred and sixty-eight feet long, and fifty feet wide. From here are five bronze doors opening into the main church. One of these doors called Porta Santa is walled up and has a cross hanging in its center. This door is broken down on Christmas eve, of the year of jubilee, which occurs every twenty-five years. The Pope commencing the work of demolition by striking the door three times with a silver hammer.

On either side of the main entrance to the church are porticos supported by four rows of marble columns between which carriages pass and repass, as well as footmen entering the church. In these porticos are quartered soldiers belonging to the Pope's guard, who are clothed in striped uniforms consisting of black, red and yellow colors, looking like a regiment of circus clowns. In the piazza fronting the church are two large fountains which are always playing, also the great

Egyptian obelisk which the ancient Romans transported from the city of the Sun more than two thousand years ago.

The prospective view of St. Peter's Church is not very imposing, as the building is on such an extensive scale that a person is apt to loose its correct proportion. The main dome which is four hundred and forty-eight feet high, and one hundred and ninety-two feet in diameter, looks neither high nor large. The marble statues of Christ and the Apostles, eighteen feet high, which adorn the front of the church, look small, scarcely life size. But on entering the church a person will be surprised at its magnitude and grandeur, which exceeds all other churches in the world, and he will find himself lost in admiration. The floor is laid with different colored marble, and the walls are composed of a like material, while the ceiling is ornamented with gilt and stucco, reminding one of Miltons description of Paradise.

On the top of St. Peter's Church is a fine walk or promenade, around the principal dome, and by the side of which are houses where the soldiers guarding the building are quartered.

In different parts of the church are sepulchral monuments to ancient popes, which contain their remains, and a statue of their person. In all parts of the church can be seen fine statuary and paintings, some of which are made by inlaying different colored marble so as to form the various shades of the picture. Among all the fine paintings and statuary in St. Peter's there is no object that attracts so much attention as Michael Angelo's statue of Moses.

In that part of the church called the Tribune is to be seen the famous chair of St. Peter, which is made of bronze, ornamented with gold and placed on the shoulder's of four colossal statues. Inside of this chair is said to be the identical one used by St. Peter, and many of his successors. In one part of the Tribune are many figures, emblems and devices, with inscriptions dated December, A. D. 1054, relating to the dogma of the immaculate conception.

Under the center of the main dome is the high altar constructed of bronze and gold, ninety-five feet high. Under this altar are the stairs leading down to the crypt, and around it is a circular balustrade composed of colored marble, on which are suspended ninety-three silver lamps that are kept burning night and day.

In five different places in the church are altars where services are frequently conducted at the same time, and around them are paintings, statuary, crucifixes, etc. Midway between these altars is the life size bronze statue of St. Peter, sitting in a marble chair, with one foot extended, and holding in one hand a bunch of keys while the other hand is raised as if he were in the act of speaking. Before this statue I saw many people kneeling in prayer, while others were kissing its big toe. Crowds of people of all classes, the ragged beggar, the soldier, the priest, as well as the fashionably dressed gentlemen and ladies, would take their turn in kissing St. Peter's big toe. First putting their lips to the toe, then touching it with their forehead, then again with their lips. On some occasions it is said that more than five thousand people kiss it in one day, and the toe is much worn by long use.

RUINS OF ANCIENT ROME.

On the south side of modern Rome, and within its walls, are still to be seen the ruins of the ancient city, consisting of palaces, temples, triumphal arches, amphitheatres and other great edifices of antiquity. Assisted by a guide, we spent some days in the examination of these ruins, visiting many of the buildings spoken of in ancient history, some of which are well preserved, and are the most interesting of all the relics of past ages.

The largest and most interesting building of ancient Rome, is the great Amphitheatre or Coliseum, which was built by the Emperor Vespasian, A. D. 72. This mammoth structure is nearly round, covering seven acres of ground, with walls from ten to twenty feet thick, and one hundred and fifty-seven feet high. About one third of the outside wall has fallen in at the top, while the remaining part is in a good state of preservation. The walls were constructed of large stone, and laid in Roman cement. On the inside of the Coliseum are many arcades or galleries extending all the way around it, and under these are dens where wild beasts were kept for the purpose of exhibiting to the public. During the first and second centuries, public exhibitions were given here, by throwing Christians into the arena of this theatre to be torn to pieces by wild beasts. History says more than one hundred thousand Christians perished in this way, and from this cause the building is now dedicated to these martyrs, and guarded by soldiers. Apartments in it are fitted up and occupied by monks, and by them public worship is held each Sabbath.

The ancient Romans believed the Coliseum would stand forever, and caused large letters to be placed over its main entrance, running thus: WHILE THE COLISEUM STANDS, ROME WILL STAND. WHEN THE COLISEUM FALLS, ROME WILL FALL, AND WITH IT THE WORLD.

A short distance from the Capitol, is an open square surrounded by buildings, and sunk about fifteen feet below the level of the surroundings. This is the site of the Curia or Senate Chamber where Julius Cæsar was assassinated (B. C. 44) and the statue of Pompey, which he fell against after receiving twenty-six stabs, is now to be seen in Spada Palace. All that now remains of that fine edifice which was the pride of the Roman Republic, is its marble floor, and twenty-one marble columns in a broken condition. On the square of the Curia, stands the tower of Trojan, eighty feet high, constructed of bronze, and is the oldest one of the kind in Europe.

On the southern slope of Capitoline Hill, among a cluster of old buildings, is still to be seen the celebrated Terperian Rock, where state criminals were put to death by throwing them off. History says Cassius was hurled down from this rock, and thus met his death in the presence of a large concourse of people there assembled.

Close by the post office in the business part of modern Rome is located the Pantheon, which was built by Agrippa (B. C. 27), and dedicated to the god of Neptune. This great relic of antiquity is now one of the principal churches of Rome, having passed from pagan to Christian form of worship, without changing its general appearance. On the front of this edifice is a wide portico supported by sixteen marble columns of fifty feet in length, and from here there is a bronze door twenty-eight feet high opening into the building. The Pantheon is round, forming on the inside a great rotunda one hundred and sixty-two feet high, with a large circular opening at the top, which is its only means of light and ventilation. And through this opening the rain has continued to pour down on its marble floor for nearly two thousand years. The inside is coated with marble, and contains many altars, paintings and statues. History says Pope Boniface IV. collected and buried under its main altar, twenty-eight wagon loads of the bones of Christian martyrs.

On descending the hill from the capitol, we entered the Grand Forum, which contains the ruins of the temples of Saturn, Concordia, and that of the twelve gods of peace. In the midst of these temples stood the original mile stone erected by Julius Cæsar, but now stands in the piazza fronting the capitol. This stone, marked the center of Rome, from which the measurement of the whole world was made. This Grand Forum at one time was the center of political strife, foreign negotiations, and commercial transactions, and from it went forth on different occasions the shouts of victorious armies. But it is now an open common, a pasture for goats, collection of filth, and surrounded by the habitations of poor ignorant lazzaroni. All those fine temples and palaces which were the pride of Rome, as well as the wonder and admiration of the world have nearly disappeared. Their marble floors fifteen feet below the street, with here and there a group of marble columns, alone remain to give an outline of their former grandeur.

From the Grand Forum we visited the temples of Jupiter and Juno, and following along the Appian Way, we came to the baths of Nero, and of Titus, as well as those of Caracalla, all of which are in a good state of preservation.

The temple of Æsculapius, is situated on an island of the Tiber, and was dedicated to the god of Medicine (B. C. 293). This temple has a curious history, with which no doubt many of the readers are familiar. Embassadors were sent to Epianrus to bring the statue of its god Æsculapius to Rome, in order to relieve the city of a plague which it was then suffering. On their return with the statue, it was discovered that a serpent had concealed itself in the ship; this they believed to be Æsculapius himself, who had assumed that form in order to deliver the city over to their enemies. On their arrival at Rome the serpent left the ship, and hid itself among the reeds of the island. And in order to appease his wrath, a temple was erected to him, the remains of which are still to be seen, and pointed out to strangers.

The largest and most important of the seven hills on which ancient Rome was built, is Palatine, where once stood the palaces of the Cæsars. Each emperor tried to excel his predecessors in the beauty and magnitude of his residence, until the whole hill became of itself a city of palaces, and the marble used in their construction has supplied modern Rome for centuries, in material for building her fine churches. Palatine Hill is about one mile in circumference, and part of the way is guarded by decayed buildings with their doors and windows filled up with brick, while the balance of the way is enclosed by a high wall. We had a great desire to see Palatine, but entrance through these walls was denied us. At last we found a lank, greasy looking fellow who had charge of one of the gates. We thought to bribe him by exhibiting money and pointing to the gate, which had the desired effect. As the great iron gate turned on its hinges, we walked in considering ourselves fortunate in seeing the palaces of the Cæsars, a privilege that few travelers have had. But great was our surprise to find before us a string of decayed buildings, extending from one side of the wall to the other, having their doors and windows filled with brick, so we could not pass through them, and instead of being in Palatine, we had only got into a goat yard. We regarded this as an outrageous Yankee trick, and turning back we tried to make the gate keeper refund the money. But he only laughed at us, pointing to the gate then to his money, giving us to understand that it was a fair bargain, and he had complied with his part of it. We all came to the conclusion that we had been nicely sold, and continued our rambles in a different direction.

CHAPTER XIII.

The city of Naples contains nearly a half million of inhabitants, and is built around the bay, which is of a circular form. The ground where it stands rises from the water's edge until it reaches the high bluffs in the rear, forming many streets which are not accessible for horses and carriages. Its streets are all flagged with lava from Mt. Vesuvius, cut in square blocks of about sixteen inches each. The city is well built with high houses, many of which are of the modern style of architecture. Some of the houses are built of white stone, others of lava, and coated with marble.

Many of its streets are of good width, kept clean, and show much activity in business. The avenue Toledo is the great thoroughfare of Naples, on which are the best stores in the city, and the crowd of people here, during business hours, is equal to the Strand of London, or Broadway New York.

On the west side of the city fronting the bay, is

a beautiful park containing many fountains and artificial lakes. And its fine walks are shaded by cypress and palm trees, among which are groups of marble and bronze statuary. This park is the great promenade of the city, where people of all classes collect to enjoy the cool sea breeze, and listen to the music from the military band.

Most of the city is well supplied with water, but in that part of it covering the bluffs, water is an article of trade, to be bought and sold same as other commodities. Water to supply this part of the city, is carried in cans on the backs of donkeys, and late and early you can hear the water sellers crying with a loud voice, *aqua eue, aqua eue.*

Much has been written about the bay of Naples. Cicero in his prose, and Virgil in his poems have lavished encomiums upon its beauty, and I believe their pictures were not overdrawn. Although the surroundings have changed, the water, islands, and mountains, remain the same as they were nineteen hundred years ago, in the days of the great statesman and poet. Cicero lived and died on the east bank of this bay, while Virgil spent most of his days on its western shore, where his tomb is still to be seen.

A person visiting Naples will see many strange things, some of which are unpleasant, and if he is not good natured, he will be out of patience much of the time. Go which way you will, hackmen are calling on you to ride, and driving their hacks in your way, compelling you to walk around them. Beggars accost you at every turn

with their dirty hats run into your face, while flower
girls are sticking small bouquets into the button holes of
your coat, in order to make a surer sale. And water
venders, with a can on their back and a mug stuck under
your nose, sing out the old familiar song of *aqua ene.*
Each morning the streets are full of donkeys loaded
with cabbage or pumpkins from the country, or returning
with manure or manufactured articles, and occupying as
much room in the street as a cart.

Morning and evening, large flocks of goats are driven
through the streets in order to supply the citizens with
milk, and at each house, a woman comes out with a mug
which is milked full by the vender. If the parties
being supplied with milk live up stairs, which is
frequently the case, in the fourth or fifth story, the
milkman taps one of the goats on the head, and starts
up stairs followed by the goat, and the milking is done
in the presence of the buyer, otherwise it would be half
water. Even then it is not uncommon for the milkman
to have in his sleeve a rubber sack filled with water,
and dilute the milk before the eyes of the buyers without
their knowledge.

The cemetery of Naples is said to be the finest in
Europe. Here millions of dollars have been expended
in building beautiful marble tombs for the rich, while
the poor are thrown into a vault, and no tomb stone
marks their long resting place. Near the center of this
cemetery is a high wall enclosing a square which is
flagged with broad stone, and contains three hundred
and sixty-six vaults for the reception of the dead, being

V

one for each day in the year. When a poor person dies, the authorities are notified, and a wagon sent to get the remains for burial, as the law prohibits a corpse being kept over night. Each night as soon as it is dark, the dead wagons come in with their loads of dead bodies, and one of these vaults is opened to receive them. By the light of a single lamp, and without mourner or friend, the burial takes place. The corpses are taken out of the wagon naked, and frequently still warm, sometimes letting the head or feet fall on the flag pavement, which reminded me of the old song running thus:

Rattle his bones over the stones,
He is only a pauper that nobody owns.

Two men take the corpse, doubling it up throw it into the vault, and as it strikes the bottom, twenty-five feet below, the sound re-echoes with a deathlike knell, that caused the cold chills to run over me. Forty is said to be the average number received daily, and after putting these into the vault, quicklime is thrown on the remains to hasten decomposition, when the vault is again closed up to be opened no more for a year.

In Naples no one can be buried in the public cemetery without receiving the rites of the church, which costs about five hundred francs, and if the dead is not worth that amount, they go into the public vaults, the same as beggars of the city. It requires nearly one hundred persons to perform the church rites, all of whom draw pay for their service. Funeral processions are seen on the street every day, at the head of which is a man carrying a long pole, capped with a crucifix. Next comes a company of priests bare headed, with the crown of

their heads shaved, which is the custom. After these
are some thirty men entirely covered with white
sheets, having a hole cut through for the eyes,
and carrying lighted candles of five or six feet in length.
Following these, is a large platform, carried by eight
men who are concealed by its gold lace drapery which
reaches to the ground. On the top of this platform is
a highly ornamented chest containing the coffin. Last
of all is a company of men, wearing a peculiar kind
of uniform, with drawn swords. Mourners and friends
never accompany these processions, all being left to
the undertakers.

One of the largest and finest churches of Naples is
called St. Genarios, being named after and dedicated to
that saint, and on that account is held in great reverence
by the Catholics. This church is coated with fancy
colored marble, both outside and in, and contains many
altars which are ornamented with paintings, statuary,
crucifixes, etc. In the crypts of the church, under the
main altar, is the chapel of St. Genarios containing
many relics which relate to the departed saint. Among
these is a glass vessel containing the ashes of his blood,
which the priests say liquifies and turns into pure blood
on the anniversary of his martyrdom, as on some other
great occasions. We said to the priest who was
explaining to us these wonderful things, that we would
like to see this miracle performed, and should be greatly
disappointed if we did not see it, as we had come for
that express purpose. To which the priest replied
"miracles were only performed by the Almighty, and

are not intended to gratify the idle curiosity of such heretics as we were."

The catacombs of Naples are the most extensive ones in Europe, and their connection with robbers, as well as the Roman inquisition, has given them great celebrity. The entrance to these catacombs is through an old convent now used for a hospital. After paying admittance fees, our party were furnished with a guide and lights to make an examination. There are three main entrances to these underground chambers, which branch off into numerous colonades or galleries of great hight and width. We passed up and down long flights of steps, into family vaults and large chambers containing various devices on the walls, showing them to have been places of heathen worship. In one of these chambers, is a round marble post where heretics were executed. Beyond this, is the chamber of death, containing a large pit where the dead bodies were thrown during the great plague in Naples, and here a large pile of skulls is still to be seen.

In the suburb of Naples, are many macaroni factories where this article is made for shipment to other countries. On visiting these factories we saw the operatives at work, almost in a state of nudity, having nothing on but a pair of short drawers. Through these factories and along the streets the macaroni was hung on poles to dry, where the dust and filth of the street are blowing constantly. After seeing the manner of making macaroni and the pranks of boys while it is drying in the street, I came to the conclusion not to indulge any more in this luxury.

Notwithstanding it was late in October, we saw many people almost naked, while at work, with their yellow skins shining in the sunbeams, which makes Naples a good place in which to study the human figure.

A VISIT TO MT. VESUVIUS.

While on the road between Rome and Naples, and about forty miles from the latter, our attention was called to the distant view of Mt. Vesuvius, which was sending forth volumns of volcanic vapors sometimes puffing like a steam engine, producing large clouds of black smoke which would shoot high into the air at each puff. It was after dark when we arrived in Naples, and the rain was pouring down in torrents. Notwithstanding the rain we found the streets full of excited people watching the great volcano, which every one thought was about going into an eruption. Flames of fire would shoot up at intervals, carrying with it large red hot stones, and accompanied by a rumbling noise like distant thunder. Although the top of the mountain is nine miles from Naples, the light from it was such as to illuminate the whole city.

From the window of my room which overlooked the bay, I had a fine view of Vesuvius, and watched it with great interest until two o'clock in the morning. About one o'clock, the mountain appeared in great commotion, sending forth flames of fire which would shoot up to a great light with a continuous roaring like the discharge of heavy artillery. At last a crater opened two hundred feet below the top of the cone, from which commenced a flow of lava that run for two miles down the mountain and appearing like a continuous sheet of liquid fire.

Two days after the opening of the crater, we made arrangements to ascend Vesuvius. Leaving Naples early in the morning, we took a carriage for Resina, three miles distant, where once stood the city of Herculaneum. This city is situated at the foot of the mountain, but eight miles from its top. Here we procured guides and horses for the ascent, and at once commenced our long, tedious journey up the mountain. For the first mile our road ran through vineyards, and fields of red peppers, the products of which are used in the manufacture of macaroni. After passing through these vineyards we came to the lava thrown out in the eruption of 1858, and for two miles traveled on it. This lava extends from the top of the mountain to the plain, a distance of six miles, destroying in its course a number of houses and vineyards, and in places it is piled up in wild masses fifty or sixty feet high. After crossing this lava flow, we came to the hermitage, which is situated on a high ridge where vegetation grows, being out of danger from eruptions. Here is an observatory built by the government for the purpose of collecting scientific information. After resting a while at the hermitage, we again mounted our horses and continued on our journey; the guides and boys accompanying us holding on to the horse's tails, to assist them up the mountain. Our appearance was extremely comical, and would have been a good subject for illustration in Harper's Weekly.

Six miles of hard traveling brought us to the base of the cone, and two miles more would take us to its top, but this had to be made on foot. Close by us was the deposit of lava as it came down the mountain in torrents, and piling up in wild masses, still red hot. Before us was the cone of Vesuvius, looking like a great black coal pit, with a smooth surface, but a steep ascent, and covered all over with lava from former eruptions. Our way was almost straight up the mountain, over loose pieces of lava, which would sometimes roll under our feet sending us backwards, and cutting our hands on the sharp crags. For two hours we plodded our way upwards, without any path, the old one having been filled up by the present flow of lava. Most of the way was close to the stream of hot lava, making the heat very oppressive. On the way up the mountain we overtook a party of Americans, two of whom were about to give out, although assisted by guides who had straps over their shoulders to which the tourists were holding on.

The scenery from the summit of Mt. Vesuvius is grand in the extreme, and which a person after seeing never can forget, should he live to the age of Methuselah. Four thousand feet below us, spread out like a map, lies the beautiful bay of Naples whitened by the sails of many nations. Upon its surface, appears to float its many picturesque islands, reflecting their image in the blue Italian sky. To the right, around part

of its circle is the great city of Naples, with its half
million inhabitants, and its many fine churches and
palaces glittering in the bright October sun. To the
left, along its eastern shore, lies entombed the ill-fated
cities of Pompeii and Herculaneum. By our side flows
a river of boiling lava one hundred feet wide, and so
red that it dazzles the eyes to look at, while two hundred
feet above us, on the top of the cone, is the great crater
blowing about once a minute, and sending forth black
smoke, red hot stones, with flames of fire. At each
blast from this crater, the noise was so great as to shake
the mountain to its very center.

Everything appeared to favor us. When we commenced the ascent of the mountain, its summit was
enveloped in a cloud, but it had now cleared off leaving
the wind in the right direction, so that we could approach
close to the crater without being affected by its heat,
smoke, or sulphureous gas. With a long pole, I took
a piece of boiling lava out of the flow, and brought it
home as a memento.

Before ascending the mountain, I felt somewhat timid,
knowing the great danger attending an ascension at the
commencement of an eruption, as no one can tell at
what time or place a new crater will open. But when
on the mountain I lost all fear, being carried away with
enthusiasm, which for the time being overruled my
judgment, and had I been alone, I should not have
lived to descend the mountain. I tried to prevail on
the guide to take me up to the flowing crater, but he
refused to go. At his refusal I lost all patience, and

called him a cowardly lazzaroni, and started up alone. I found myself within twenty feet of the crater, the heat burning my hands and face, but before I had time to make a survey of its contents, the guide had hold of my arm, pulling me away. And it was well he did so, for at that moment the big crater above, blew forth showers of stone, which fell on the spot where I stood. In my anxiety to view the flowing crater, I had forgotten all about the blowing one, and had placed myself between the two. My guardian said afterwards, if I had been lost, it would have injured his reputation as a guide. This he no doubt thought of more consequence than saving my life.

The flowing crater as near as I could judge, was about one hundred feet wide, with the bank on the upper side of it, rising about twenty feet, while on the lower side, the lava was flowing off like a waterfall, boiling and hissing as it went. The many stories told about looking down into the crater, and its being a deep vortex of liquid fire, is without any foundation in fact. The crater when flowing is always full of lava, and is like a pot boiling over, but when it stops flowing, the lava cools in it, and nothing is to be seen of it after- wards, it being the same as other parts of the mountain.

The big crater on the top of the cone is always open but never throws out any lava, and when the mountain is not in eruption it is quiet, occasionally smoking and hissing. But when eruption takes place, according to scientific observation, the whole mountain rises, and the crater expands until it becomes a great vortex of an

W

immense width, and probably many hundred feet in
depth. I have conversed with different guides about
this crater, but could obtain no reliable information; each one only giving his opinion, as no person
can approach close enough to make any observation.
Even when the mountain is not in eruption, it is unsafe to go close to it. Last summer an English sea
captain venturing too near the crater among the ashes
and cinders he slipped into it and was never seen
afterwards.

We had all seated ourselves on the lava, some distance from both craters, and were having a fine social
chat with our new-made acquaintances who were all
Americans, when the big crater gave one of its terrific
blows, which appeared to shake the mountain to its
foundation, and at the same time two heavy raps were
felt under us. We all jumped to our feet in great
alarm, thinking that a new crater was about to open
where we sat, and commenced a hasty retreat down the
mountain. With us was a tall, lank, greasy looking
fellow, who had carried up the mountain a basket of
wine and eatables, which he expected to sell to us at
extravagant prices. But when he found our party
about to leave without buying his provisions, he went
into a terrible way. With curious jestures and loud
talk which none of us understood, he placed himself
in our way and tried to make us stop. Our guides who
expected a part of the treat, said there was no danger,
as thumping in that way, was very common. But
being panic struck, there was no stopping us, and we

continued to retreat in bad order, until we reached the base of the cone.

It was long after dark when we reached Naples, being much fatigued with my journey, and my hands bleeding in many places from being cut on the lava, but I was highly pleased with my visit to the great volcano.

CHAPTER XIV.

HERCULANEUM.

Three miles from Naples, and under the flourishing town of Resina, lies entombed the ill-fated city of Herculaneum. Many will recollect reading an account of the destruction of this city, as well as Pompeii, given by Pliny the younger, who was an eye witness to it, and his account is the only written one on record. This account says: "It was in the afternoon of August the 23d A. D. 79, when darkness enveloped the bay of Naples. The sea receded a great distance, leaving the ships in the harbor out of water, then came back with a loud roar, smashing to pieces the shipping, and washing houses off the shore. All eyes were turned towards Vesuvius, which was sending forth flames of fire, and roaring with such terrific force as to drown all other noise. And from it came forth a torrent of lava which covered up the city, filling the bay for a long way."

For near seventeen hundred years this city was lost

from sight; even tradition failed to point out its exact location, until parties at Resina discovered its ruins by accident. There is but a small portion of these ruins open for inspection, although the work of excavation has been going on for a long time; the greater portion of it has been filled up after removing its treasures.

On going into the office of Herculaneum, which is located on a business street of Resina, we bought tickets, and were furnished with a guide and lights for a descent into the city below. After going down two long flights of steps which were cut out of lava we came to the upper tier of seats belonging to the great theatre. From here we descended to the stage, which has a marble floor, and surrounded by beautiful marble columns. Next we went into the dressing room and examined the marble statues, and fresco paintings on the walls. On leaving the dressing room we passed out into the street and examined the pavement, which is composed of blocks of lava like the streets of Naples. This theatre is much larger than those now in use, and was a building of elegance and beauty. It is now eighty feet below the streets of Resina, being covered over with lava, which is harder than ordinary rock.

The treasures taken out of Herculaneum are to be seen at the Naples museum, which consist of statuary, paintings, mosaic work, and almost everything used by people at the present day. I saw steel safes much like those now in use, as well as nearly all kinds of implements used in mechanical art. Here are gold rings with diamond sets, and various kinds of jewelry that might be taken for the most fashionable patterns. One room in the museum is occupied by a library taken from the ruins, and consists of seventeen hundred volumes, all in rolled manuscript, a few of which are unrolled so as to exhibit the writing. Here are to be seen a number of mummies wrapped in their wearing apparel which has become petrified by the chemical effects of the lava.

There are seventeen apartments in the museum, filled with articles taken from the ruins, and contain many remarkable things. Among other curiosities is a small bronze profile or medallion of St. Paul, with his name in Latin, *San. Paulus Apostolus.* Since my return home I have seen photographs of this medallion, sold through the country, and purporting to be a genuine likeness of the Apostle. This representation is not improbable, as it is well known that the destruction of this city was only eleven years after the apostle's death, and other things, are found among the ruins which show that Christians were living in the city at the time of its destruction.

RUINS OF POMPEII.

These ruins are eight miles from Naples, one and a half from the bay, and five miles from the cone of Vesuvius. On the morning of the 22d of October, we left Naples in a carriage to visit the ruins' of this great city of antiquity. The road leading to it follows around the bay, through a number of towns which join each other in close succession, making it difficult to tell where one

ends and another commences. In one of these towns
named Poctici, we saw large piles of lava, fifty feet or
more in hight, and the streets in many places were cut
through them.

According to history Pompeii at one time was the
greatest commercial city of southern Italy, carrying
its commerce on different seas, and its ships were seen
in every port; but it now lies entombed sixty or seventy
feet under ground, where it has slumbered for near
eighteen hundred years. Although excavations have
been going on for more than a century, only about one
third of it has been resurrected, the remaining portion
is covered with earth, on which are vineyards and
cultivated fields.

Pompeii was a seaport, but its harbor was filled up at
the time of its destruction, and now are cultivated farms
where once floated merchant ships. Herculaneum was
covered with lava, but Pompeii appears to have been
covered with dirt which was blown from the mountain.

After paying the usual fees at the gate of Pompeii,
we were furnished with a guide, who conducted us
through various parts of the city, and pointed out, and
explained many things of interest. The streets are
very narrow, paved with square blocks of lava, and are
much worn by carriage wheels. Many of the streets are
not wide enough to admit of carriages passing each
other, and at the crossings, are placed large square
blocks of stone between which the carriage wheels pass.
Most of the houses are built with lava, and coated with

stucco, which gives them the appearance of marble.
The upper part of the buildings appear to have been
thrown down at the destruction of the city, leaving only
the first, and in some places the second stories standing.
Our guide first conducted us to the two theatres, then to
the barracks where sixty-three dead bodies were found.
Next to the house of Marcus Lucretius, who was according to history a Roman senator, and a man of great
wealth. This is the house so often referred to in a book
entitled, "The last days of Pompeii." Fronting the
main entrance of this house, is lettering on the sidewalk made by inserting pieces of colored marble forming
the name and title of the occupant. The floors of this
house are composed of marble, and the walls of
many of its rooms are covered with beautiful fresco
painting, with the colors as bright as if only done the
day before. In the open court are still standing many
marble statues, and the remains of a fountain surrounded
with marble columns, showing it to have been a place
of great splendor. We next visited the Grand Forum
which contains the ruins of the temples of Fortune,
Jupiter, and Venus, also the Tribune, Senate Chamber,
with many other buildings of a public character. The
floors of these buildings are made of white marble, and
groups of marble columns in a broken condition are still
standing.

Between the Grand Forum and the gate Isis, are the
remains of a heathen temple, which contains an altar in
the form of a serpent. Around this altar are many

fresco paintings on the wall representing forms of heathen worship, one of which shows a priest offering up sacrifices to an unknown God.

Many of the houses in the business part of the city have signs above the door consisting of a figure of the articles made or sold within. Some of these signs are made of crockery, while others are cut out of stone, and mostly contain the name of the firm. Here are houses of ill-fame, with signs above the doors, and the walls of the principal rooms are covered with obscene fresco paintings of life size. In the cellar of one of these houses were found twenty-seven skeletons; on some of which were gold bracelets, and diamond rings. One of these skeletons had a key in one hand, and a bag of gold in the other.

On the west side of the city, the excavation has been carried up to the city walls, and in one place two hundred yards beyond it. Passing out at the Herculaneum gate we followed along the Appian Way, by many beautiful monuments, until we came to the palace of Diomedes. This is a building of great beauty, excelling in magnitude and grandeur, any of the villas of the present day. In the open court of this villa are the remains of a fountain surrounded by marble columns and statues. Near this fountain is a bath house, constructed of marble, and containing many articles of furniture. After going through many rooms of this palace, we went into the wine cellar which consists of four wide alcoves, each of them being one hundred feet in length. Here are many earthen vessels for

x

holding wine, some of which are capable of holding many barrels. On the fatal night, the inmates of this palace, seventeen in number, took refuge in this cellar where their bodies were found in a good state of preservation; five of whom were found leaning against the wall, and the alluvium hardening on their bodies,'left their impression which is still to be seen. One of these bodies was that of a boy, whose flaxen hair still cleaves to the cemented wall.

Near the center of the city is the museum of Pompeii containing many curiosities taken from the ruins, and consisting of almost every variety of articles now in use. All kinds of metals are black, and vegetable matter looks like charcoal. Here are to be seen wheat, potatoes, coffee, figs, apples, olives, and loaves of bread with the baker's name stamped on them. And here in a glass case are five petrified bodies, one of which is of a woman with a gold ring on one finger.

Our guide conducted us through long streets, narrow alleys, dark and ill-ventilated buildings. Then into fine palaces, over marble floors, among beautiful statuary, and fresco paintings. We almost imagined at each turn, that the proprietors of these buildings would meet us and seek redress for trespassing on their domicil. But in these buildings, and along these streets no human being is seen, or voice heard; all is still and lonely. Eighteen hundred years have passed away since the citizens of Pompeii ceased to exist.

After spending many hours in rambling through the city our guide told us that his time was up and he could go no farther. We asked the privilege of remaining longer, to continue our rambles without him; but our request was denied, by saying that no persons are allowed to walk the streets of Pompeii, unless accompanied by an officer.

When our sight seeing was at an end here, we left this part of the city, taking with us in a carriage the guide, to show us the amphitheatre, which is situated in the south-west part of the city, and is the only building excavated in that direction. This building is not so large as the Coliseum at Rome, but nevertheless is a mammoth structure, built in a circular form, and containing thirty-five tiers of stone seats.

Tradition says, on the day of the destruction of Pompeii, many thousand people were collected in this ampitheatre to see the play, and were thus better able to make their escape, than from the more crowded parts of the city.

SOUHERN ITALY.

At Naples we went aboard of a steamship for Calabria and Sicily, stopping at a number of places along the southern coast of Italy. The country in the south part of the peninsula is mostly mountainous with here and there a fertile plain. Many of these mountains are barren and rocky without timber or vegetation of any kind, while on the more fertile slopes, the olive, grape, and fig, are cultivated. Most all the towns along the coast are without harbors, and large vessels are obliged to lay at anchor some distance from shore, and freight and passengers are taken back and forth in row boats. When the sea is rough, the transit is made with great difficulty, and sometimes is impossible.

The people here appear to lack the enterprise and intelligence of those living in the north part of Italy. Many of them are brigands, or outlaws, and obtain their living by robbery. Forming themselves into banditties, they roam through the country in search of spoil, always accompained by a priest, who absolves them from the sin of robbery. Part of this country is unsafe to travel in. A short time ago an Englishman was captured by these brigands, within eight miles of Naples and twenty thousand dollars were paid for his ransom. The government is making an effort to break up these bands, and a large military force is employed for that purpose. At Salarno eight hundred of these robbers were in prison, and others were brought in daily.

In the poorer parts of the city, as well as country villages, are found a class of people called lazzaroni mostly wearing red knit caps, dirty greasy roundabouts, and exhibiting bare mahogany colored legs. These people appear to be a degraded race, possessing but little physical or mental power, and are lazy and indolent living principally on fruit and macaroni. Many of whom are theives or beggars.

The Italians appear to have less scruples in point of honesty than other people in Europe. With a stranger who cannot speak their language, they will take every advantage. In a number of cases, I bought railroad tickets above the established fare, leaving a few francs for the agent to put into his own pocket. But on detecting the swindle, and going back to the ticket master, he would disgorge. This they will do readily when caught.

There is no country in Europe, where a person can travel so cheap as Italy, if he understands Italian usage; otherwise he will find it most expensive. In stopping at a hotel the price of room, meals, service, candles etc. should be agreed on beforehand, otherwise it will be double price. I have seen shrewdness among hotel keepers in Italy, which cannot be surpassed by the Yankees of America. On the arrival of trains or steamers, cabs loaded with travelers will go around to different hotels, until they can suit themselves with good rooms and cheap fare. The landlord or clerk will show the newly arrived guest a large well furnished room with two or more beds, and the price reasonable. But before the arrival of the next train, the landlord tells the occupant that a number of guests have arrived, which makes it necessary to have his double room. Consequently the occupant is taken to a small room in the attic, leaving the large one for the next guest, who is tricked the same as his predecessor.

At a hotel in Messina where I stopped, I noticed on the arrival of each train or steamboat, a number of fine looking girls, wearing short green jackets and white lace caps, standing in the court of the hotel. These girls would make themselves very agreeable to strangers, bowing and smiling gracefully, sometimes opening the door of cabs, to assist the guests out, and their politeness would cause many to stop, who intended to seek quarters elsewhere. In all my travels I have not met with a man so old or so much devoted to grace, as not to be influenced by a pretty face, and if undecided which hotel to stop at, this would always settle the question.

The girls seen at this hotel belonged to a sewing establishment on the adjoining block, and were employed by the landlord to visit his hotel on the arrival of each train and steamboat.

CHAPTER XV.

This island is mostly mountainous, with many fine valleys, and in places are extensive table-lands on the tops of mountains. It has but one short railroad, and but few carriage roads, consequently traveling is mostly done on the backs of mules or donkeys, and like southern Italy is full of brigands, which makes it unsafe to travel through. Oranges and lemons are raised extensively in the valleys, while olives, grapes and figs, are grown among the mountains. And these articles constitute the principal exports of the country. .

Messina is one of the largest cities of Sicily, containing over one hundred thousand inhabitants, and is situated at the head of the strait bearing the same name. It is well built, and has a fine harbor with a circular wharf. From here there is a railroad running down the coast to Catania, sixty-four miles distant, being the only railroad on the island. Along this road are many beautiful orange and lemon groves, where fruit is grown for foreign shipment. Here are farms fenced with cactus, which grows about ten feet high. Many miles of this road is cut through lava which has flowed from Mt. Ætna, and in some places the road is tunneled under mountains of it. While on this road the cars stopped at a small town, where a large crowd of people had collected, all of whom appeared much excited. A number of guns were fired, and a ball from one of them passed through the window close to my head, and knocked the hat off a man sitting next to me. Not understanding the language, we could not learn the cause of this excitement.

CATANIA.

The city of Catania contains seventy-five thousand inhabitants, and is situated at the foot of Mt. Ætna, from whose eruption it has been partly destroyed a number of times. The city has many wide and straight streets, and the houses are built with lava, many of which are faced with marble or coated with stucco. Near the center of the city are the ruins of two large theatres, one of which is an amphitheatre, now covered over with lava sixty feet deep, and houses built thereon. Conducted by a guide with lighted torches, we examined these ruins, which show the fine mechanism of former ages. We passed through dark arcades, up and down steps, along the seats of the galleries, on the stage, and in the dressing rooms. Here are many fragments of statues and columns, all of which are composed of

Grecian marble. At what time these buildings were destroyed is not known, but it is thought to have been before the Christian era.

Here in Catania as well as other cities of Sicily, much of the trading and mechanical work is done in the streets. Blacksmiths, shoemakers, and tailors, as well as women sewing and spinning were seen at work along the public thoroughfares. In the streets and public squares, men are seen with a table and writing materials, whose business it is to write letters for people, as the mass cannot write, consequently have to depend on these scribes to carry on their correspondence.

Caravans of donkeys loaded with wine from the country are seen on the streets every day with their large demijohns on either side of them. As they pass through the gate of the city, the custom house officers take out the cork of each of these demijohns, and smells its contents to see if they contain whisky or brandy, as these articles are liable for duty.

In the west part of the city is the *piazza a donne*, or wash square, where the women of the city collect to do their washing. Here are many large stone tanks through which the water runs, and at all times of day a large collection of women are seen washing, many of whom are standing in water above their knees with their clothes fastened around their waist. The manner of exposing their person would be revolting to women of the United States.

Here at Catania, Mt. Ætna is in plain view, and can be seen from its base to the top of its cone, and appears

Y

close by, although its summit is sixteen miles distant. Part way up its slope is a belt of forest trees, above which is a bare rocky surface covered with almost perpetual snow. A large portion of its slope, as well as the plain for many miles below is covered with lava piled up in wild masses, and in some places the sea for a long way is filled with it.

At Catania we boarded a steamer for Syracuse, thirty-six miles down the coast, and saw its beautiful circular bay which has been so often referred to by ancient writers of Greece and Rome. The ruins of the ancient city of Syracuse cover a large space of level land, on which are parts of temples, and palaces, with groups of marble columns still standing. The temples of Minerva and that of Venus, so highly spoken of by Cicero are still to be seen in a state of ruins.

Modern Syracuse stands close by the ruined city, and contains some twenty thousand inhabitants, and is strongly fortified.

After remaining here one day, viewing the ruins of this great city of antiquity, we again went aboard of a steamer bound for Malta.

THE MURDERER.

A short time before my arrival in Catania, Sicily, a murder of a revolting character had been committed. A man by the name of George S. Mason had murdered his mistress, for which he was arrested, convicted, and condemned to die. Mason formerly lived in Chicago,

where he was engaged in commission business, and by
which he accumulated a large fortune. But getting
into trouble through some of his business transactions
he left the country to escape criminal prosecution. In
his flight he was accompanied by a girl of respectable
parentage, from a neighboring town. This young and
confiding girl under the promise of marriage, left her
home, forsaking her fond parents and kind friends, to
follow the fortune of a man who was unworthy of her
confidence.

Mason and his pretended wife, traveled over a year
on the Continent, spending much of their time at fashionable watering places. At Baden Baden I frequently
saw Mason gambling, and he continued at the table until
he was a ruined man. From Baden Baden he went
to Sicily with the expectation of procuring an agency
of the New York and Italian transportation company
which had commenced about that time to run a line of
steamships, partially for the purpose of carrying fruit
from Sicily. Failing in this, and being without means he
became desperate, and determined to rid himself of his
pretended wife, so as to raise money on her jewelry to
carry him out of the country. And believing that death
to her would be better than abandonment in a strange
land, he committed the act for which he was about to
suffer.

Back of Catania, and part way up the eastern slope of
Mt. Ætna is a cliff of rocks, rising almost perpendicular
for several hundred feet in hight, on the top of which
is a table rock projecting over and forming a precipice.

From this point the view of the surrounding country is very fine, overlooking the city and Mediterranean sea for many miles. On the right, the mountain slope is covered with pine trees, while on the left, the mountain and plain below are covered with lava, where it has been accumulating for thousands of years.

It was late in the afternoon, as Mason and his mistress stood on this rock, with their opera glasses viewing the ships far out at sea, when he caught her around the waist and threw her off. Her mangled body fell from crag to crag until it landed lifeless and bleeding upon the rocks below. As I looked on the stains of blood which were still visible on the rocks, I thought of her with an angelic form, beautiful black curls, the gayest of the gay whom I had seen a few months before at Baden Baden, while promenading with her reputed husband. But here in a foreign land unknown, and without friends, she met her death at the hand of him who was pledged to protect her. At the time of the murder a party of English tourists were descending the mountain, and hearing the girl crying for help came in sight as she was hurled from the rock. For this crime Mason was arrested, convicted and condemned to death.

Four days previous to the time set for Mason's execution, I went to his cell and learned from him many of the facts above narrated. I found him standing by a small grated window, with his hands and feet in irons and chained to the floor. He appeared glad to see me, and while speaking of his fate, the tears followed each other in close succession down his cheek.

On that bright October morning as Mason stood looking through the grated window upon the shipping in the harbor, and the smooth sea, beyond, I thought how eagerly he must wish that he was once more innocent and free, with years of life in prospect, instead of the four short days that lay between him and eternity. Notwithstanding he was a murderer of the blackest dye, I could not help sympathizing with him, and for the time being almost forgot the cold brutality of the crime and only thought of the ruined condition of the man.

I left Catania the next day, and learned nothing more about Mason, but in all probability he met his fate according to the decree of court.

MALTA.

Midway between the coast of Europe and Africa, is situated the island of Malta, a place of great historical celebrity. This island is fifteen miles long, eight miles wide, and elevated high above the sea. It is barren and rocky, without forests, and some parts of it without vegetation of any kind. Having two days of spare time here, we hired a carriage to ride over the island, and visited a number of interesting places. On high land elevated more than one thousand feet above the sea, and near the center of the island is located the old city of Cita Vecchia, the former capital of Malta. This city contains many interesting ruins, among which are the temples of Juno and Neptune, and near them are extensive catacombs. From this city the whole of the island is visible, presenting a large district of table-land partly covered with rocks, while here and there are seen green pastures, orange groves, and cultivated gardens.

On the north-west coast of the island, is a small inlet surrounded by rocky bluffs, and called Port of San Paulo. Tradition says that it was here St. Paul landed after his shipwreck, as he was being conveyed a prisoner to Rome. A monument is. erected here to commemorate that event.

Valetta, the principal city of Malta is built on a slope of rocky bluffs with one street rising above another. Many of these streets are ascended by stone steps, and are not accessible for carriages. The city is built of white stone, and has a clean attractive appearance, containing many fine churches, some of which were built by the Knights of St. John. It has a fine harbor which is always full of ships. Sail vessels frequently make into this harbor to avoid storms and sea, and steamers stop here for coal. There is a large British garrison here, and the harbor is strongly fortified, being one continuation of batteries on both sides of the harbor, some of which are cut out of the solid rock.

The Maltese are large robust people with copper colored skin, and their dialect is peculiar to the island, being a cross between the Italian and Arabic. I saw in the harbor a Maltese diver who was exercising his skill for money. As people would throw a shilling into the water, he would dive after it, sometimes catching it before it would reach the bottom.

PERILS AT SEA.

At Malta we took passage on a French mail steamer for Alexandria, Egypt, nine hundred and fifty miles distant. On the second day out, we encountered a terrible storm which continued for two days, causing much distress and sea sickness among the passengers. Those on deck were brought down into the cabin, filling its floor with sick women and children, while the sea at intervals would break over the ship flooding the cabin with water. On the deck of the steamer were a large quantity of hogsheads filled with American kerosene oil, some of which broke loose from their fastenings and tumbled about the deck over the fire. If one of these had bursted, nothing could have saved the steamer from burning, when all on board would have been lost.

Captain Anderson formerly commander of the Great Eastern, also of Atlantic cable celebrity, was on board of this ship as a passenger. He remained on deck all one night, assisting in the managing of the vessel, and prevailed on the captain to turn her off the course, which in all probability was the means of saving the vessel, as well as the lives of the passengers. Captain Anderson said to me afterwards, had he known that there was kerosene oil on deck, he would not have gone aboard of her, and he considered it almost a miracle that she was not lost.

The ship being overfreighted, acted badly in the

rough sea, and was in danger of being swamped. The captain thought it best to make for the island of Candia, which lies towards the Grecian coast, but after running in that direction one day, the wind calmed and she was again headed towards Alexandria, which place we reached on the sixth day. The passengers expressed much joy at the sight of land, and many of them declared that they would not go to sea again in a steamer that carried kerosene oil on deck.

GENERAL REMARKS.

Having traveled more or less in most all of the principal countries of Europe, I had a good opportunity of learning something of the customs and habits of the people. In the better sections of country, people live with that ease and comfort seldom enjoyed by people in the United States. The country being already made by their ancestors, and all that is required of the present generation is to obtain a living, leaving the remainder of their time for pleasure seeking and enjoyment of life. With the better class there is an air of politeness and refinement seldom met with in the United States. In the northern countries especially in Holland, it is a universal practice for men to take off their hats when meeting a friend, and a failure to do this is considered a breach of good manners. In Prussia and Italy it is common for men to kiss each other when meeting or parting. I have frequently seen men with long shaggy

beard take a cigar out of their mouth and kiss a score
or more of their male friends.

Wine and beer are drank extensively, but drunken
persons are seldom met with. During eight months
travel on the Continent, I saw but two drunken persons.
If drunkeness exists here, it is kept in-doors and
not seen in public places. People do not chew
tobacco, but smoking is of universal practice, and
allowed in most all public places, such as dining rooms,
railroad cars, court rooms, etc. In most of the first
class hotels one or more of the employees understand
English, but people speaking English are seldom met
with in the rural districts. Many of the educated
people of the different countries understand French, and
if a tourist can speak that language he will have but
little trouble in any part of the. Continent.

In cities on the British Isles, drunkeness, poverty, and
low sinks of vice, meet the eye of a tourist, at almost
every turn, but they are seldom seen in cities on the
Continent. The principal cities on the Continent
employ but a small police force, still life and property
are more secure than elsewhere, and a person can pass
through the public streets without fear from cut-throats
or pick-pockets.

z

CHAPTER XVI.

ALEXANDRIA.

We had been six days at sea while making a passage from Malta to Alexandria, when it was announced at the mast head that land was in sight. Every glass aboard of the ship was brought into requisition, when far in the distance could be seen the African coast rising only a few feet above the water. Further on we came in view of the city of Alexandria, with its harbor full of ships, presenting a forest of masts. Among these ships were seen the steam fleets of the British, French, Austrian, and Turkish navies.

The city of Alexandria is built on level land, which is elevated but a few feet above the Mediterranean Sea, and is partly surrounded by water. It contains one hundred and twenty thousand inhabitants, about four fifths of whom are Arabs. Most of the streets are narrow, not exceeding twelve feet in width, unpaved, without sidewalks, dirty and filthy. Many of the streets are partly filled up with tradesmen's stands, donkeys, camels, and dogs which makes it difficult to pass through them. A few streets only are wide enough for carriages to pass. Along these, and on Frank Square are many stores kept by Europeans. The houses are mostly built of gray stone, arched over at the top and coated with cement. The streets, with a few exceptions, are without lights, and most of the houses have no windows in front, to throw light on the street, consequently they are dark and gloomy after night.

Water to supply the city is brought from the Nile by means of a canal forty miles in length, and it is kept in underground reservoirs which were built more than two thousand years ago. Instead of the water being conducted into various parts of the city, by means of hydrant pipes, it is carried through the streets in goat skins on the backs of donkeys.

Packs of large hyena like dogs that have no master, and governed by no law except their own brutal instinct are seen every where on the streets acting as public scavengers, and are all the while barking and snapping at people as they pass. At night these dogs collect on the public squares, and make night hideous with their howling and fighting.

Every half hour during the night a call is made by the chief policeman, which call is taken up by other policemen and sounded all over the city. Each morning at daylight watchmen on the minarets of all the principal mosques, with a loud voice call on the people to come for prayers.

The ancient city of Alexandria was founded by

Alexander the Great (B. C. 330), and was intended for the capital of his vast empire. For many centuries it was the great center of wealth, commerce, and literature, and the whole world paid it homage. Of this great city, but little is now to be seen, and its pomp and grandeur exists only in the history of the past. Unlike Rome and Syracuse, where ruined temples are still to be seen, and are the wonder and admiration of the world. With the exception of a few monumental obelisks and broken columns scattered among Arab hovels and palm groves, nothing can be seen above ground to mark the location of this great city of antiquity. Where workmen were engaged in excavating for a railroad, fifteen feet under ground, I saw pieces of beautiful Corinthian columns and marble house floors, and for some ways the foundation of this railroad has been cut through basements of ruined buildings.

CURIOSITIES OF ALEXANDRIA.

On a gravely knoll outside of the city limits, stands Pompey's Pillar, which is considered one of the great curiosities of Egypt. This is a round shaft composed of one solid piece of red granite, smooth and highly polished, eighty-five feet long, and twenty-nine feet in circumference. It stands on a square base or pedestal twelve feet high, making the whole hight of the shaft ninety-seven feet. But little is known about the history of this great monument of antiquity. Tradition says that it stands on the spot where Pompey was beheaded, and was erected to commemorate that event. But writers on antiquity discard this tradition, but fail to give the world any satisfactory history of it.

Within the city limits and close to the old harbor is Cleopatra's Needle, another relic of past ages. This is a square shaft of red granite, eight feet square, and seventy-one feet high, tapering towards the top and is covered with Egyptian hieroglyphics. Close by this shaft is another obelisk lying down, and partly covered up with sand. Many years ago the authorities of Egypt gave this obelisk to the British government, but it probably will never be removed to England.

On a projecting point of land extending into the sea near the light house, once stood the great Egyptian Pharos which is spoken of in the ancient history, as one of the seven wonders of the world. This structure consisted of a tower built of white marble and so high that the beacon lights on its top could be seen one hundred miles at sea. History says this tower was erected by order of King Ptolemy three hundred years before Christ. The King caused his name to be engraved on it as savior gods, the great benefactor of mariners, and by it he intended his memory should be perpetuated to all time. But the builder wishing to secure the glory to himself, engraved his own name on the stone, then covering it over with stucco on which appeared the name of the King. In time the stucco fell off and with it the King's name, leaving the builder's in its place. We visited the site of this great tower and saw pieces of its ruins scattered over the stony knoll and along the beach of the sea.

A short distance below the commercial part of the city overlooking the harbor, is located the royal palace, and close by it is the royal harem. These, buildings show much skill in their construction, combining European with Oriental style of work. The Grand Pacha or King of Egypt lives in Cairo, where he has a palace and harem, but these buildings are for his entertainment when he visits Alexandria. We were not allowed to enter the harem, or harem grounds, and consequently know but little about its internal arrangements, but I understand that it contains about fifty women who are under the guardianship of a eunuch. These women are from different countries and of various colors, from the fair Circasian girl, to the coal black Nubian, with a few European women, and two Yankee girls from the United States.

ROAD TO CAIRO.

Our stay in Alexandria was a short one, and early in the morning of November the sixth, we were on the cars for Cairo, one hundred and thirty miles distant.

The railroad which connects these two great Egyptian cities, was built some years ago by the English East India Company. The embankment on which the road is laid, is raised high above the floods of the Nile, and the management of the road is much the same as those in Europe, having three different class cars.

The ride through the country was a delightful one, being over a level plain by the side of fields of waving grain, and through green pastures on which were feeding large herds of sheep, goats and buffaloes. Although it was November, farmers were engaged in cutting wheat and rice, while the corn crop was not more than half matured. In a number of places I saw people cutting grain where the water was standing two inches deep all over the field, not yet having evaporated from the late inundation.

After a few hours ride we came to the Nile, the sight of which created among the passengers a great enthusiasm, many of whom on looking out of the car windows would sing out: The Nile, The Nile.

This great river of Africa has long been a mystery to the world, and its waters in ancient times was considered a specific for all maladies. For more than one thousand miles of its length it receives not a single tributary, but rolls on through this great valley, by its seven mouths emptying its turbid waters into the clear blue sea. A river which was worshiped by the ancient Egyptians, and whose great size astonished the Greeks and Romans, and whose overflow was to them a profound mystery.

The railroad crosses on stone bridges, four different branches of the Nile, being below the point where it separates to form its numerous mouths. While on the road, but twenty-two miles away, we obtained our first view of the pyramids, which looked at that great distance like a cluster of hay stacks. At last we came in sight of Grand Cairo, with its eleven hundred minarets glittering in the bright afternoon sun. On arriving at the depot we found ourselves surrounded by a motly mass of human beings consisting of beggars, dragomans, donkey boys, and dancing girls. But crowding our way through these human leeches, we found quarters in the Grand Hotel d'Europe.

NILE VALLEY.

The valley of the Nile in places is fifty or sixty miles in width, and is a rich level plain elevated but a few feet above the Mediterranean Sea. At Cairo the valley is only eight miles wide, but above and below, it spreads out into a vast plain. The desert lying on either side of the valley is a barren elevation consisting of hills and dales with plains of sand and hills of rock without water, grass, or vegetation of any kind except here and there a bunch of willows about two feet high.

The Nile at its annual floods rises about thirty feet overflowing the country and causing this vast plain to look like a great inland sea, dotted over with towns and villages. The inundation generally takes place early in July, and subsides by the last of August. The river Nile has low banks, an even current, and its waters are always muddy, having a dark chocolate color, but when it settles, it is clear and sweet, and from it the whole country receives a supply of water for drinking, washing, etc.

Canals are made everywhere through the Nile valley, carrying water on to every farm, from which the land is irrigated. At the annual rise of the Nile, these canals fill with water, which remains all the year, supplying the inhabitants with the necessary fluid. If the floods are not sufficiently high to wet the more elevated portions of the land, the deficiency is supplied by artificial means, which is mostly done by men raising water with swinging buckets. Rain seldom falls in Egypt and unless the land is watered, it bakes and is unproductive. In this great valley there are neither springs, rivulets, brooks, nor running water of any kind, except the Nile. Where wells have been dug, the water is found to be so impregnated with saline matter as to render it worthless even for steam purposes.

The soil consists of a rich black loam producing fine crops of various kinds of grain, such as wheat, corn, rice, cotton, and sugar cane. Corn is planted the last of August, and matures in December. Wheat is sown in November, and harvested in March. Two crops of wheat a year are frequently raised off the same land; the last crop is harvested in the fall.

Within the last few years a number of English capitalists have been engaged in the culture of cotton and in many of the towns along the Nile, the smoke can be seen rising from their steam cotton gins.

A.*

CHAPTER XVII.

GRAND CAIRO.

The city of Cairo, the capital of Lower Egypt, is situated on the east side of the Nile, and one hundred and forty miles from its mouth. It is said to contain about four hundred thousand inhabitants, most of whom are Arabs and Mamalukes. Much of its commerce is carried on by Greeks, Turks and Jews, with occasional English and French merchants. At a distance the city has a very imposing appearance, with its four hundred mosques, each of which has from two to six minarets, or spires, causing it to look like a city of churches. A few streets in Cairo are wide enough to admit carriages one of which called Muskay, is thirty-two feet wide, and along it are the principal bazars and wholesale stores of the city. The buildings on this street are high and in places poles are placed on their tops reaching across the street, and supporting a covering of reeds, so as to protect it from the scorching rays of the sun.

The streets of Cairo will not average more than nine feet

in width, and are so crooked and winding that a person cannot see more than ten rods along them. The houses are constructed of white stone, and built projecting over the street, forming dark arcades where the sun never shines. Windows of the upper stories are mostly ornamented with lattice work, projecting over the street, and in some places the windows of the opposite house are so close that a person can step from one building to another across the narrow street. The houses are flat on the top, being covered with stone and cement, and on the roofs of some of them are summer houses, play grounds for children, etc. In many places the streets are arched over with massive stone walls, and houses built thereon. Gates are placed at each end of many of the streets, which are locked at night. In these streets are stores, or trading posts and where people eat and sleep, same as in houses.

On a high knoll overlooking the city, is located the Grand Mosque, which for beauty and magnitude excels all other buildings in the city. Before entering this mosque we were provided with slippers, so that our boots might not defile the holy place. The floor is covered all over with beautiful brussels carpet, but contains no seats, as the form of Mohammedan worship will not admit of any. The day of our visit to this mosque, was the Mohammedan Sabbath, (Friday with us), which gave us a good opportunity of seeing the manner of worship. During preaching the congregation were seated on the floor, with their feet under them like a tailor on his bench. After preaching they stood some time in prayer with their hands raised above their heads and their faces turned in the direction of Mecca. Then they would kneel down, lean forward, and kiss the floor. There were no women in the mosque, and I am informed that they never attend public worship.

After spending some time in the mosque we visited the Royal Palace which is close by, and walked through the richly furnished apartments of the Grand Pacha. We next went into the court of the citadel which is memorable for the murder of the Mamaluke Beys, in the year 1811. We also examined the old breach in the outer wall, where Emin Bey jumped his horse over, and thus made his escape, being the only one out of more than four hundred victims.

On the bank of the Nile, some ways from the crowded part of the city, is located the grand Egyptian museum containing many curiosities taken from the pyramids, with a great variety of strange things which belonged to the ancient Egyptians. Near this museum is still to be seen the ruins of an old theatre, where the Turkish Sultan, Selin I., in the year 1517, caused thirty thousand prisoners to be beheaded in his presence, and their bodies thrown into the river.

Outside of the city limits and in a beautiful palm grove, was being held at the time of our visit an Egyptian fair, which is conducted on the same plan as the Dutch fairs of Europe. The amusements at this fair were of a low order, some of which were on the juglar plan and were disgusting to look at. Here was an old Arab with two fat daughters and two trained bears.

The girls were dressed to imitate the bears and the bears to imitate the girls. When they came on the stage to dance their manner of jumping up and down and rolling over each other was such as to make it difficult to distinguish the girls from the bears.

In another part of the fair ground was a Nubian negro, exhibiting a big snake, a real live African boa constrictor of twenty-five feet in length. With this snake he would perform many strange feats which were frightful to behold. One of which was pulling open its mouth with his hands, to exhibit its teeth and its long forked tongue.

STRANGE SIGHTS IN CAIRO.

The streets of Cairo present a singular appearance; no omnibuses, wagons, or drays are seen, but a motly mass of human beings, crowding their way through the narrow alleys some on foot, others on donkeys. Men with long gowns wrapped around their bodies, and long Turkish pipes in their mouths, are seen cantering their donkeys to and fro. Women with masks over their faces, riding astride, followed by a boy carrying a stick to guide and whip the donkey, are seen crowding their way through the narrow streets. At almost every turn of the street we encountered caravans of camels loaded with building materials, produce, or boxes of dry goods. On the great thoroughfares of the city, we would occasionally meet a carriage containing a man of distinction, or women of the royal harem, always preceded by a footman to clear the way. These footmen are dressed in a white frock, with a red sash over their shoulders, and in their hands they carry a long pointed staff, like a barber's pole. This staff they flourish over their heads, and yell at the top of their voices, notifying people to get out of the street, so the carriage can pass.

Water to supply the city is carried through the streets in goats skins, which are tanned with the hair on, and strings tied around the neck and legs to make them water-tight. This kind of water cask is used in all the cities of the Orient, and when lashed on to the back of a donkey, looks like a dead hog.

Funeral processions are frequently seen on the streets, and their doleful funeral dirge can be heard above all the other noise of the great metropolis. These processions are always preceded by two men carrying the coffin on their shoulders, and are followed by a retinue of priests chanting at the top of their voices. Next comes a company of weeping women, who are covered up with long black robes, and their weeping and wailing exceeds anything that I have ever heard. These women are employed as public mourners, but their cries and lamentations appear genuine. If the deceased was rich, a camel goes before the procession, loaded with bread and wine, to be distributed among the attendants at the grave.

Almost every day we met marriage processions, attended with loud shouting, clapping of hands, and bands of music. The bride on her way to the place of marriage is mounted on a camel, and entirely covered up with a large silk robe. Four men carry over her head, (suspended on long poles), a canopy made of silk, and ornamented with gold lace. Accompaning these processions are men engaged in all kinds of gymnastic feats, and fighting sham battles to amuse the people. With these processions are also troops of singing and dancing girls, who are beating on drums, tin pans, and playing on various kinds of musical instruments.

Many of the dry goods stores are not more than eight feet square, and all open to the street. The merchant is in the inside of his store, while his customers are on the outside. Here you will see a blacksmith at work sitting cross-legged on the floor with his anvil before him, and his bellows by his side. Next a money changer, out in the street with his safe by his side, and scales to weigh the coin. Then a scribe with a stand on which are writing materials, who is always ready to exercise his skill in writing letters or contracts.

HOWLING DERVISHES.

Conducted by a dragoman carrying a lantern, we left our hotel at ten o'clock at night, to witness the wonderful performance of these religious fanatics. On our way we were obliged to pass through a number of streets which are always locked at night, but by giving the gate tender plenty of backsheesh, we were allowed to pass. The streets through which we passed are not more than eight feet wide, and partly filled up with salesmen's stands where goods of various kinds were lying around on tables and shelves unguarded. Many people were asleep in the streets, having retired for the night, and occasionally we would tramp on their toes, or stumble against their heads, which would bring from the sleeper a hoarse growl.

On arriving at the place of howling Dervishes, which is in the rear of the great Dervishes mosque. We were admitted into an outer court of a large hall, by paying two shillings each. The main part of this hall was filled with Arabs, who were almost in a state of nudity, Their long shaggy beards, and smoothly shaved heads caused them to look like imps from the infernal region. The exercise for the evening had already commenced and the worshippers would kneel down to kiss the floor, then standing up with their hands raised high above their heads, they would yell at the top of their voices, Allah, Allah. After going through with this exercise, the dancing and howling commenced, and exceeded anything of the kind that I had ever seen or heard before. The performers would jump up and down in quick succession with their mouths open, tongues hanging out, and uttering the most unearthly yells, worse than a bedlam of howling lunatics. Some would spin around like a top, while others would jump, hop, and skip around the room with their long, yellow, half naked bodies jerking and wriggling in a horrible manner. At the same time they would howl so loud and so coarse that the braying of an ass or roaring of a lion would be music to it. Many of the performers soon became too much exhausted to hop, and too much out of breath to howl, but would sway to and fro frothing at the mouth, and occasionally uttering a hoarse growl. After the performance had continued for some time, the voice of the howlers lost all semblance to that of a human being, consisting of a hoarse smothered grunt which appeared to come from the pit of their stomach.

When the howling was over, a low sob was heard in one part of the hall, then another, and another, until the whole party were crying at the top of their voices, filling the room with loud bursts of wailing.

It was now after midnight, and the exercises not yet over, but we had seen enough of the howling Dervishes, and we left for our hotel. But we all came to the conclusion that this performance exceeded all other strange things which we had seen in Grand Cairo.

DONKEYS, AND DONKEY BOYS.

The donkeys of Egypt are very different from those of Europe, having more life, and activity, and are not that dull, stupid animal found in other countries. It is said that these donkeys are of a different race, being the descendants of the wild ass of Tartary or Circassia, of which the patriarch Job says, is of God's noble work. Shakespeare in his delineation of the human character says, an honest man is the best piece of divine production. Which is right in their declarations, I will not pretend to say, as it would be a delicate matter to decide on points controverted by these great

B*

authors. Whether the man or the ass is entitled to superiority in creation is not material to this subject. But it is very certain that no animal in Egypt is of so much service to its owner, as the donkey. Here they pay a triple debt, acting as horse, carriage, and dray. For the saddle they are preferable to the horse, and for light packages they are better than the camel. Large droves of them are seen in the streets, carrying produce or merchandise, stone, or mortar for building purposes, and water to supply the city. If a cellar is to be dug, a large drove of them are seen carrying dirt, going back and forth to the place of loading and unloading, without a driver.

In the streets of Egyptian cities, tourists are all the while annoyed by donkey boys, with " Will you have a donkey, good donkey, gallop all day and never fall down, very cheap, etc." Thus they will continue to praise their donkey, not forgetting to tell that he is named for some great man in America or England. It is difficult to get rid of these boys, as they will continue in your company, leading their donkey in the way, so that you will have to walk around it. The donkey boys, (many of whom are grown men) do not lack in shrewdness. They understand the way to drive a good trade, and can talk almost any language to suit their employers. When they let their donkey, they always go with it, carrying a stick to guide, and whip it when necessary. These boys appear to have great endurance, and will follow a donkey when on a good gallop for many miles, without showing much fatigue.

CHAPTER XVIII.

GOING TO THE PYRAMIDS.

On the evening before our intended visit to the pyramids, I told some donkey boys that a number of their donkeys would be wanting the next morning at the Grand hotel d'Europe, and long before we were up a large drove of them were in waiting for us. The donkey boys who were full grown Arabs, had many of their donkeys named after distinguished men of England and America, but would change their names, at any time, to suit French or German customers. Next came the selecting of such of the donkeys as we thought would suit our purpose. I selected one called Yankee Doodle, which proved to be an excellent animal, and I rode him every day during my stay in Cairo. In our party was a Presbyterian clergyman from Philadelphia, by the name of W. H. Martin, a man of much piety, who frequently reproved some of the company for using bad language. In selecting our donkeys the parson made choice of a large, gray, mule-headed stallion, called

Andy Johnson, saying at the same time that he not only liked the looks of the donkey, but his name was a great favorite with him.

All things being ready we started for the pyramids which are eight miles distant. The boys running after us and whipping the donkeys into a gallop. On we went through the crowded streets of the city, sometimes among caravans of camels loaded with stone, or long building timbers, which caused us to dodge our heads this way and that to prevent collision.

Before leaving the hotel, one of our party learning the tricks of Andy Johnson, gave the boy having him in charge a shilling to have him show off at the parson's expense. Scarcely had we passed the city limits, when the donkey on receiving a signal from his master commenced jumping up and down, and kicking at a furious rate, acting much like a trained mule. The parson tried to quiet him by kind words, which were first spoken in English, then in French, but the donkey understanding nothing but Arabic, continued to kick and jump, until he landed his rider headlong into a dirty place in the road. At this turn of affairs, the parson lost all patience and gathering himself up, with his hands and face all covered with filth, he gave vent to some hard words which he afterwards proposed to take back. But we said to him that he ought to take nothing back, as he was justifiable in all that he had said, and even then he had not done half justice to the case. If this paragraph should ever meet the eyes of friend Martin, it is hoped that he will pardon me for letting the world know that he was in any way connected with the tricks of Andy Johnson.

Things being again righted, we continued on our way with the donkeys on a gallop, and the boys running after them with their petticoats flying above their knees. We passed many beautiful groves of palm trees, and by the side of cultivated gardens, and green pastures, making the ride a delightful one. Three miles travel brought us to Old Cairo, where we crossed the Nile in a sail ferry boat.

Before reaching the pyramids we were met by about twenty Arabs, who turned back and went with us, for the purpose of selling mementos. These Arabs belonged to the pyramids, and were large athletic men speaking good English, and whose wearing apparel consisted of a turban and a white cotton frock coming down to their knees, leaving their feet and legs bare. About one mile from the pyramids, we came to a bayou caused by the rise of the Nile. Here we left our donkeys, and after being ferried over this bayou, we continued our way on foot. On our road we had to cross a slough of a few rods in width, and agreed with the Arabs to carry us across for a sixpence each. Gathering their skirts under their arms, they carried us across in quick time. Two of them took me up exclaiming at the same time: "Oh very heavy, worth a shilling." When part way across they stopped, one of them, pretending to stick fast in the mud, and saying: "Too heavy, will you pay a shilling." I replied no, go on, and thinking of being on a balky horse, I commenced kicking. The nails in the heels of my boots coming in contact with their bare hips made some red marks, for which they claimed a sixpence damage. However they carried me over safe, and I paid them a shilling, believing it to be cheap enough.

PYRAMIDS AND SPHINX.

The pyramids of Gizeh are the largest, and the most celebrated of all the different groups in Egypt. These are located at the west side of the Nile valley, and at the edge of the desert, where the sand is all the while drifting around them. There are three pyramids in this group, the largest of which is called Cheops, being four hundred and fifty-six feet in perpendicular hight, and covering an area of nearly thirteen acres It is built of large blocks of stone, from two to four feet thick, and about twenty feet in length. It is a square mass of stone, and rises on either side like a flight of stairs, with an average of four feet base, and three feet rise. Near Cheops is a pyramid called Cephrenes which remains perfect at the top, running up to a sharp peak and coated with colored marble. By the side of these two pyramids is another one of much smaller dimensions which completes the group.

At what time, and for what purpose, and by whom these pyramids were built, writers on antiquity do not agree.

Close by the pyramids, and partly covered up with drifting sand is seen the great Sphinx, the ancient

Egyptian god. This great relic of antiquity is constructed of red granite, representing in its formation the body of a lion, with a head of a man, and is in a crouching position. Its body is one hundred and twenty-eight feet long, with the head rising fifty-five feet in hight, and measuring around it eighty-nine feet, while its enormous paws stretch out in front of its breast, fifty-seven feet.

By the side of the Sphinx are the ruins of the temple of the Sphinx, which have of late been brought to light by the removal of sand. This temple is shown to have been a building of elegance and beauty, being surrounded by finely carved columns, while its walls and floors are composed of colored marble.

THE ASCENT OF CHEOPS.

At the pyramids we were surrounded by about thirty Arabs, all anxious to bargain with us for making the ascent, but we would make no contract with them until we had seen the Sheik, who is the man in authority, being governor of the village. Our dragoman brought the Sheik to us and we agreed with him to furnish us the necessary assistance for four shillings each, without any backsheesh.

All things being ready, we commenced the ascent of Cheops with four Arabs assisting each of us, two pulling at the arms, one pushing at our back, and the fourth following after to render any assistance necessary. Long before we had reached the top, our conductors became clamorous for backsheesh, which is money in addition

to that agreed on, but we refused to give them any
until they had completed their contract. After a
fatiguing journey of nearly half an hour, including
many resting spells on the way, we reached the summit.

The view from the summit of this pyramid is very
fine, presenting a beauty of landscape scenery, probably
unequalled in Egypt. Below us is an Arab village,
around which are seen remains of earth fortifications,
where in 1797 was fought the battle of the pyramids, in
which Bonaparte defeated the Mamaluke Beys.

The Nile for many miles could be seen with its
numerous bayous and lakes, caused by the late inunda-
tions. To our right lay the ruins of Memphis, once the
home of the Pharaohs, with its five pyramids which
look in the distance like huge hay stacks. To our
left we could see the city of Cairo, with its four hundred
mosques and countless minarets glittering in the sun
beams. Behind us lay the great desert, with its mountains of rocks and plains of sand. But we were not
allowed to enjoy this beautiful scenery, for the Arabs
continued to hound us for money, trying to make
us buy their trinkets, which they said were antique,
being found in the pyramids. But knowing it to be a
criminal offense everywhere, to sell a genuine article,
I ridiculed their statements, by saying that the Yankees
in America made those things by steam power, and sold
them for three shillings per hundred. At my declara-
tion they laughed heartily, and gave a loud cheer for
the Yankees of America, after which they sang the
jolly song of Yankee land.

On the top of the pyramid is a level space of some fifty feet square, showing that many feet of its top has been taken off. Here on the top are large stones, ten or twelve feet in length, giving to it the appearance of a native quarry; and on these are cut many names of visitors, also the United States flag painted in red, white, and blue.

After descending from the pyramids, we prepared ourselves with lights, to enter its vaulted chambers, which is a severe ordeal to accomplish on account of bad air and dust.

For some ways we went down an inclined plain through a dark dusty tunnel where we had to go half bent. Then up steep steps, and through a narrow passage where we almost crawled on our hands and knees. At last we entered the grand hall, and from there we passed into the king's and queen's chambers. These are large apartments, but the account which I read, describing their beauty and magnitude is very much exaggerated.

Our sight seeing at the pyramids was now at an end, but our troubles were not, for the Arabs had collected around us in a threatening manner, demanding more money. We gave them additional four shillings each, but this only made them clamorous for more. For protection we appealed to the Sheik and his military guard, which consisted of only one man, who was armed with an old flint lock musket, that looked as though it might have been used at the taking of Jericho. But we found these officials to be the greatest robbers of the gang, and for a time our case looked desperate. I gave

c*

the military guard two shillings to protect me from further annoyance from these robbers, which he did faithfully, and as they collected around me, he would go at them with his long, rusty musket and push them away. While in the midst of confusion we, left the pyramids, followed by the Arabs yelling for backsheesh and rallying in our front, in order to make us stop. At last we came to where we had left our donkeys, and mounting, we put them in a gallop for Cairo, feeling much relieved in ridding ourselves of the Arabs; but it had cost us about ten dollars each, to see the pyramids.

A VISIT TO THE PETRIFIED FOREST.

We left Cairo early in the morning to visit the petrified forest, which is situated in the desert, about six miles from the Nile valley. The first object on the road that attracted our attention, was the tombs of the Caliphs, the former kings of Egypt. Each tomb is covered by a large Turkish mosque, with many tall minarets. They stand on the desert a short distance from the city, where the sand is all the while drifting around them, and have a dilapidated, forsaken appearance. Farther on we came to large stone quarries, where the stone was obtained to build Cairo, and here camels were being loaded with building stone. A railroad is now being built to these quarries which will obviate the slow process of packing stone on camels. This petrified forest which has for many years attracted the attention of men of science, is located on high land, which is covered with sand and rocks. There are no trees here but pieces of petrified wood, three or four feet in length are seen scattered over the ground. These pieces of wood show the growth of the tree, knots, hearts, and parts of limbs. There are many acres of ground covered over with petrified wood, and containing pieces of almost every size and shape, all of which have the appearance of limestone. If I did not have the opinion of geologists, and other men of science who pronounce these rocks, petrified wood, I would be led to believe them only a curious formation of stone.

As we were returning from the petrified forest, my friend M. Mauley met with quite a mishap, which caused much merriment among our party. The donkey on which he was riding becoming tired of carrying two hundred and twenty-eight pounds, over rocks and through the burning sand of the desert, thought it best to ship his burden, and down he came with his nose, as well as that of Mr. Mauley in the sand. In this position both Mr. Mauley and the donkey lay, until we dismounted and picked them up. All things being again righted, we continued on our way, but the donkey repeated his tricks three or four times, finally breaking Mr. Mauley's spectacles, and barking his nose as it came in contact with the sand.

HELIOPOLIS, OR CITY OF THE SUN.

Accompained by an intelligent dragoman, we made a visit to the ruins of this ancient city, which is situated eight miles north-east of Cairo. According to history the city of the Sun, or Heliopolis, was the oldest and largest of all the ancient cities of Egypt, and was a place of great wealth and splendor. The remains of the temple of the Sun, with a few fragments of broken columns, together with a standing obelisk seventy-two feet high, are all that now marks the spot where stood a great city of antiquity.

From Heliopolis, the ancient Romans transported the mammoth obelisk now standing in front of the church of St John Laterena, Rome, also the one in the piazza of St. Peter's church.

Near the ruins of the city is a spring shaded by a large sycamore tree, and under its shade were found collected a large number of Arabs, some of whom were praying or singing psalms, while others were smoking their pipes. This spring is said to be the only one in the Nile valley, and is known as the fountain of the Sun. Tradition says, when Joseph and Mary with the infant Christ visited Egypt, they encamped at this spring, and caused its bitter water to be pure and sweet.

In the vicinity of this ruined city, are many beautiful palm groves, and the trees at the time of our visit were loaded with fruit. The palm groves of Egypt are said to be unequaled in any other part of the world. The trees here grow from fifty to sixty feet in height, the trunk retaining its size to the top. On the top of the trunk is a cluster of limbs turning downwards like a weeping willow, between which hang large bunches of dates of one hundred pounds or more each.

On our return to Cairo, we saw an early piece of corn partly destroyed by the wild boar. These animals live among the rocks of the desert, far away from human habitation, from which they come forth at night to destroy the growing crops, to the great annoyance of the farmers.

MEMPHIS, OR NOPH OF SCRIPTURE.

Twelve miles above Cairo, and on the west bank of the Nile, are still to be seen some of the ruins of Memphis. This city was the former capital of Egypt and home of the Pharaohs' as well as the residence of Joseph and Moses. But it has long since disappeared, leaving only a few relics to mark its location, and to give an outline of its former greatness. Here are five pyramids and a Sphinx, as well as remains of ruined temples and palaces. In different places are mounds of earth containing pieces of pottery and scraps of broken marble columns. With other relics of antiquity, is a colossal statue forty-two feet long, cut out of limestone, and is supposed to represent one of the ancient kings of Egypt. This statue has been broken off from a pedestal where it once stood, and now lies partly buried up with mud and water.

Occupying part of the site of the ancient city, is now a miserable Arab village, surrounded by fields of corn, cotton, and sugar cane. The boundaries of the ancient city of Memphis, as pointed out by the Arabs, are large enough to have contained over one million of inhabitants and over a large portion of this ground not a vestige of its ruins are seen. The buildings having been constructed of unburned brick, long since mouldered into earth, while the marble of which its fine temples and palaces were composed, has been removed to build modern cities.

The prophet Jeremiah in speaking of this city says: "Noph shall be waste and desolate, without an inhabitant." How well this prophecy has been fulfilled. Where once stood this great city of the Nile, are now palm groves and cultivated fields, among which scarcely a vestige of its former grandeur remains.

Two miles below Memphis is a small bayou in the river with its edges covered with bulrushes. This is pointed out as the place where Pharaoh's daughter found Moses cradled in an ark.

OLD CAIRO, AND ISLAND OF RODA.

Old Cairo is situated on the west bank of the Nile, three miles from Grand Cairo and is said to occupy the site of the ancient Egyptian Babylon. Here are the remains of an old Roman fortress, built nineteen hundred years ago. Some of its towers are still standing, on one of which remains the Roman Eagle. One of these walls contains a curious device, representing Deity sitting on a globe which is supported by two angels. In the upper part of the town near the river, is an ancient

THE NILE AT OLD CAIRO.

structure called Joseph's granaries. Tradition says, it was in these buildings that Joseph stored the corn, in providing for the days of famine.

Here in old Cairo, we visited an Egyptian grain market, which is situated out of doors, and on a public square. The different kinds of grain were lying on the ground in large piles, between which is a public thoroughfare for the passage of camels and donkeys. The grain is kept in this way at all seasons of the year as rain is almost unknown in Egypt.

In the river below the town is located the beautiful island of Roda, which has been so often referred to at different periods of Egyptian history. This is a small island with grassy banks and shade trees, on the upper end of which stands the celebrated Nilcometer. This is a square stone building, containing a stone pillar, having on it scales and figures to show the rise and fall of the Nile. At the time of annual floods, criers on the minarets of all the principal mosques in Grand Cairo, inform the people night and morning of the rise or fall of the river as shown by this pillar.

The accompanying picture shows the manner of ferrying the Nile, with the island of Roda in front, and the pyramids in the distance.

ARAB LIFE IN THE COUNTRY.

Having traveled several hundred miles through the Nile valley, I enjoyed an opportunity of learning many things relating to the customs and habits of the people, social life in the rural districts, manner of farming, etc. In the country the masses are poor, and inclined to indolence, but in every village there are one or more persons of wealth, the owner of farms and herds, on whom the poorer classes are dependent for employment. The title of the land is in most cases, in the hands of the government, and each occupant of a farm pays high rent for its use. All kinds of property are taxed at a high rate, even the palm trees, and all other trees bearing fruit are subject to a special tax. When the crops are light, many of the farmers are unable to pay their taxes, and their property is sacrificed. In addition to the sacrifice of property, the delinquent tax payer receives one hundred lashes on the bottom of his bare feet, providing the tax collector believes that proper means have not been used to obtain the money.

There are but few horses or cattle in Egypt, camels, donkeys, and buffaloes supplying their place. Plowing is mostly done with buffaloes, and it is not uncommon to see a camel and buffalo yoked together before a plow.

In Alexandria and Cairo, there are a few carriages, but carriages are not found in other parts of Egypt, as there are no roads on which they could run. All kinds of produce, merchandise, lumber, stone, etc., are carried through the country on the backs of camels and donkeys. In all the principal cities there are hotels kept by Europeans, but they are not found in other parts of the country, and if a traveler wishes to stay all night in the rural districts, he is entertained free of charge by the

Sheik of the village. The expense of traveling in Egypt, is about double that of Europe, and the hotels charge by the day, instead of the restaurant plan of Europe. A tourist will find less trouble about language here, than on the Continent. The French language is the best for Europe, but English is the best for the Orient.

In Egypt there is neither wood, coal, nor peat, and the fuel used here by the natives, is made out of manure, mixed with cut straw, rolled out into thin cakes, and dried in the sun. This kind of fuel is an article of trade, bought and sold in market, and is carried through the country on camels and donkeys, the same as other commodities.

D*

CHAPTER XIX.

The inhabitants of Lower Egypt are principally Arabs and Mamalukes, and are of all shades and colors, from the fair skinned Circassian, to the jet black Nubian. In the rural districts, but few Europeans are found, but in the cities many different countries are represented. In the country, people live in villages which are located on the highest ground, so as to escape the floods of the Nile, and at a distance these villages look like a cluster of hay stacks. The houses are constructed of mud or unburned brick, and are one story high, without chimney, window glass, or door shutters. In the middle of the roof is an open dome, through which the smoke escapes. In these houses they have no bedsteads, chairs, nor tables, but sleep on mattresses placed in one corner of the room, and they sit on the floor after the fashion of a tailor on his bench. Neither do they use knives and forks, their place being supplied by fingers. Many of the people sleep out of doors; while passing through the streets early in the morning, I saw many lying by the side of houses, with their heads covered up, while their feet and legs were bare.

The people are mostly educated, and are very religious, spending much of their time in prayer and singing hymns. By the side of mosques, as well as by the wayside, are stone pillars called praying posts, where people are seen at all hours of the day standing in prayer. On the top of these praying posts is a directory, pointing towards Mecca, so the persons praying, may have their face turned in the direction of that holy city. The Arabs carry their religion into their business transactions, and have a low opinion of the honesty of Christians. I have talked with different ones on this subject who say, if they go to a Mohammedan merchant, they will get full weight and measure, but with a Greek, (Christian,) they are apt to be cheated.

The dress of the men, consists of a blue frock, coming down to their knees, leaving their feet and legs bare. On their head they wear a knit turban, wrapped around with many folds of white cloth. They wear their beards long, but shave their heads once a week. I have frequently seen men at work in the field while in a state of nudity, many of whom were over six feet in hight, and of various shades and colors.

The women wear a long gown, made mostly of blue cotton cloth, with a shawl over their heads, and are generally barefooted, and little appreciating the troubles of Flora McFlimsey. They frequently stain their lips and teeth with hanna, giving to them a blue color.

Many of them have their hands and face tattooed in blue colors representing various patterns and styles, which are made in conformity to the goddess of fashion. They wear a mask over their face, consisting of a thick, black, knit scarf, extending down to their heels, and looking at a distance like an elephant's trunk. In these masks are holes for the eyes, and a gold ornament on the ridge of the nose.

At a station north of Cairo, thirteen women dressed in long silk robes, and belonging to a rich man's harem came into the cars and took their seats in that part of the car designed for harem women. While on the road the door of their apartment became partly ajar, and sitting close by, I saw these women, who were of differing colors, with their masks off so as to smoke their cigarettes. But when they saw me looking at them, they gave a loud scream, and covered their faces with their masks. At this alarm, a eunuch who had them in charge, came and closed the door.

ARAB MARRIAGE CUSTOM.

Having conversed with different Arabs regarding their marriage custom, I find that it is nearly the same as laid down in the Mosaic laws. A woman among them is not won in courtship, but purchased from her father and is an article of trade, the same as a donkey or camel. Every man, rich or poor, has to buy his wife, and he is governed in quality according to the extent of his purse. The price of wives varies according to the state of the money market, but fifty dollars is about the average. Girls of great beauty, or having a father in high position, will sometimes bring five hundred or one thousand dollars. A man having marriageable daughters, will sometimes sell them to men who will give the most money, without consulting the girl's wishes, frequently to old men to supply their harem. A man having sons, will lay up money to buy them wives, and if a young man has to rely upon his own resources, he will save every penny for that purpose.

A donkey boy over six feet in hight, whom I frequently employed, said to me, that he had no father to buy him a wife, consequently had been saving money for that purpose. He told me that one Mr. Turner of New York, whom he had served many days, bought for him a coat and a pair of boots, being the only ones he ever had, but said that he could not afford to wear them, so he sold these articles, and laid by the money to buy him a wife. I said to this donkey boy, if he would go to America, he could obtain a wife without buying, to which he replied: "They certainly could not be worth much, if obtained in that way."

Men sometimes marry a wife without having seen her previous to the wedding day: all arrangements being made by the fathers of the parties. On the wedding day the bride, attended by friends, is placed on a camel covered all over with a silk robe, proceeds to the residence of her intended husband, where the marriage takes place, and the purchase money paid to her father. I have frequently seen these wedding

parties passing through the streets of Oriental cities
attended with loud cheering, clapping of hands, bands
of music, and troups of dancing girls.

If the wife at any time proves unfaithful to her marriage vows, the injured husband claims of her father the
return of the purchase money, and if the evidence of the
bride's purity is not shown at the time of marriage, the
money paid for her is also refunded. A man can put
away his wife at any time, without showing cause for it.
All that is required for a divorce, is a public announce-
ment in the church. Men can have as many wives as
they wish; most rich men keep a harem attended
by a eunuch.

Women among the Arabs do not occupy that high
position in society which they do in more civilized
countries. Here they are regarded as inferior to men,
and are seldom seen in public accompanied by a male
friend. A man would as leave be seen in public with
a stolen sheep on his back, as in the society of his wife.

SUEZ CITY.

Some years ago the East India Company built a railroad directly across the desert from Cairo to Suez, a
distance of ninety-six miles. But this road has of late
been discontinued on account of drifting sand filling up
the track, and a new one built, which runs down the
Nile valley for forty miles, then across the desert to
Suez, along the fresh water canal. This road runs

about eighty miles on the desert, and in many places
guards are placed by the side of the track to prevent
the drifting sand from filling it up. At many of the
stations on the desert, people live in tents, not having
had time to erect buildings.

The city of Suez is built on a sandy flat, near the
head of the Red Sea, and is partly surrounded with
water. It is said to contain a population of twelve
thousand, beside a large number of wandering Arabs,
generally encamped in its suburbs. The streets are
without pavement or sidewalks, being a continuous bed
of sand, in which a person sinks at every step. The
houses are built of stone, flat on top, covered with
broad stone and cement, not generally water-tight, but
rain is almost unknown in Suez. Houses in some places
are built compact, so that a person can walk a long ways
on their tops. On many of these houses are goat and
poultry yards, play grounds for children, and also praying posts, where the heads of the family go night and
morning to pray. The streets of the city are full of
dogs, donkeys, and goats, and contain filth of every
description, producing a great variety of offensive smells,
thus making Suez the most repulsive place that I have
found in all my travels.

There is neither grass, trees, shrubbery, nor vegetation of any kind around Suez, and there is no farming
land within seventy miles, being surrounded by a sandy
desert. Every article consumed here comes from a
distance. Even the water to supply the city is brought
by means of a canal from the Nile, ninety miles distant,

and carried through the streets in goat skins and sold to the occupant of each house.

Suez is on the high road to India, and every steamship that sails up the Red Sea, is filled with passengers for Europe, when a special train is fitted out to carry them to Alexandria.

RED SEA.

At Suez, we crossed the Red Sea in a sailing vessel, and examined the mouth of the great ship canal, then being built to connect the water of the Red Sea with that of the Mediterranean. And from here we walked for some distance along the sandy shore of Arabia, shading ourselves with umbrellas, as the heat of the sun was very oppressive, although late in November. While here, I encountered a gale of sirocco, or poisonous wind of the desert, which effected my health for some weeks afterwards.

Some distance below Suez is the place located by tradition, where the Israelites under the leadership of Moses, crossed the Red Sea. At this point the sea is about one mile wide, and on the Arabian side the beach is flat, with shallow water, while on the African side the water is deep, and the shores are bounded with peaks of mountains. An eminent writer says this place is the only one which accords with the Bible account of this miracle. Other writers locate the place near the head of the gulf where the water is more shallow, and contend that the Israelites crossed at low tide, while the flow destroyed Pharaoh and his host, thus doing away with the necessity of a miracle. Reading these different opinions caused me to spend some time in the examination of these places, and I am satisfied that the latter opinion has no foundation in fact. The water on the east side is shallow, but on the west it is deep, and vessels drawing fifteen feet of water pass over it, even at low tide.

On the African side of the Red Sea, is a rocky, barren mountain called Jebel Attaka, from which it is said Mt. Sinai can be seen, although a long way off. We ascended this mountain, which gave us a fine view of the sea and surrounding country, while far to the south-east, we could see the blue outlines of a mountain which the Arabs say is Sinai, but those better acquainted with geography, say it is Mount Catherine, which is closer by.

The shores of the Red Sea, and country adjoining it, present a scene of barrenness and desolation probably unequalled on the face of the Globe. Neither verdure, grass, nor trees are seen, nor one green spot on which the eye can rest, but a continuous mountain of rock, or plains of sand.

ISTHMUS OF SUEZ.

A short distance north of the head of the Red Sea, is the great highway across the desert connecting Palestine with Egypt. Over this road in all probability the sons of Jacob passed when going to Egypt for corn, and

E*

it is equally probable that Joseph and Mary with the infant Christ traveled it, when fleeing to Egypt to escape the persecution of Herod. On this road are seen large caravans of wandering Arabs, and pilgrims going to, and from Mecca.

Across the isthmus of Suez, is the great ship canal, to which I just alluded. This canal is eighty-four miles long, three hundred feet wide, and intended to be twenty-six feet deep, and when completed ships will pass through it directly from Europe to East India. We traveled along the whole length of this canal. On the east part of it were many steam excavators engaged in removing dirt and rocks. On this canal midway between the two seas, is a new town called Ishmalia, and by its side is an artificial lake of about one mile in diameter, filled with water from the Mediterranean Sea. Thus a commercial city is being built in the middle of the desert, and the rattling of cars, and puffing of steamers are now heard on these wild, sandy plains. At Ishmalia we went aboard of a small steamer running on the canal to Port Said. On our way we passed a large number of steam dredging boats employed in deepening the canal, and removing drifting sand, which is all the while blowing into it.

Port Said is a new place, situated on the Mediterranean at the mouth of the canal. It is located on a narrow neck of land, extending into the sea, and its site is principally made of dirt, which was dredged out of the bay in making its harbor. It is now a place of great commercial importance, having already taken much of the East India shipping business away from Alexandria. Port Said like Suez, has not a tree, or grass plat within fifty miles of it, being surrounded by a level sandy plain, which rises only a few feet above the sea. The water to supply the city, comes from the Nile, being taken out of the fresh water canal forty miles west of Suez, and from here it is brought forty-four miles in iron pipes.

At Port Said we went aboard of a steamship for Joppa, Palestine, nearly two hundred miles distant.

CHAPTER XX.

On the morning of the nineteenth of November our ship, after buffeting the wind and waves all night, came to anchor at Joppa. Here there is no harbor, and the coast is full of rocks, consequently large vessels are obliged to lie at anchor about half a mile from shore, and passengers and freight are carried back and forth in row-boats. When the sea is rough, the transit is both difficult and dangerous, and frequently passengers and freight for Joppa are carried by, it being impossible to land them.

As soon as our steamer came to anchor, she was boarded by a large number of Arabs, grabbing hold of baggage, and quarreling among themselves, as to who should have the largest share of passengers. The sea was very rough, causing the row-boats to toss up and down at a fearful rate, putting us in great danger of being swamped; this, together with the quarreling of the Arabs, made the debarkation the most disagreeable part of my travels.

On reaching the wharf, we found it crowded with half naked, barbarous looking Arabs, who were anxious to assist us in getting upon the pier, so they could claim backsheesh. When landed, we were surrounded by twenty or thirty of these leeches, all of whom claimed money on the ground of having assisted in pulling us up on the pier. We gave some of them small pieces of money, but this only made them clamorous for more. These Arabs followed us into the custom house, and along the streets, yelling at the top of their voices. One of them more daring than the rest, struck an Englishman in our company, on the head with his staff, and in return, one of our party pointed a revolver at them, which caused them to leave us in quick time, when we continued on our way.

CITY OF JOPPA.

The city of Joppa, (now called Jaffa,) is built of white stone, and stands on a knoll, with the streets rising one above the other. It is said to contain about twelve thousand inhabitants, most of whom are Arabs. From the sea the city has a bold and imposing appearance, but on entering, all of its romance disappears, and a person will find its distant view was very deceptive. The streets are only about eight feet wide, many of them quite steep, being ascended by stone steps. In some places the streets are arched over, and houses built thereon. Dirt and filth of every description abounds in the streets, and droves of loaded camels are passing and repassing through these narrow thoroughfares, causing people to stand up against the houses to prevent collision with them.

We are told by writers on antiquity that no city in Palestine has undergone so little change as this, and Joppa to day is much the same as Joppa of two thousand years ago. In former times, it was the principal seaport of Palestine, and it is so now. In the days of Joshua it is spoken of as a maritime city allotted to Dan, and many references are made to it, both in the Old and New Testaments. It was here Jonah took shipping for Tarshish, was shipwrecked, and swallowed by a great fish. Here, by the seaside, lived one Simon, the tanner, who entertained Peter. We visited the house said to have been Simon's, and found it close by the light house, where the waves were beating against the rocks at its base. This house is now unoccupied, but its stone floors, massive walls, and arched ceilings remain perfect. We ascended to the top of the house, which is flat, being covered with large flag stones, and stood where Peter is said to have been when he saw the vision. If this is not the house once occupied by Simon the tanner, it answers well its description, and looks as though it might have been built long before his time, and I see nothing to prevent its standing for two thousand years to come. Some may think it improbable that a house would stand for so long a period, but I have seen houses in the Jewish quarters of Rome, still occupied, which were built before the Christian era.

Outside of the walls of Joppa, and in a beautiful orange grove, is located the American Colony, which settled here a few years ago under the supervision of the Rev. Mr. Adams. Their houses are constructed of wood, painted white, and were shipped from Boston on the same vessel that brought the emigrants. This colony is not in a flourishing condition, many having returned to the United States, and those remaining are dissatisfied with the country, and intend to return also. Among those remaining is a man by the name of Rolly Floyd, who is now engaged in running a hack between Joppa and Jerusalem, and he claims the honor of introducing the first, and only vehicle into Palestine.

In the vicinity of Joppa are many beautiful orange groves, the finest that I have met with, in all my travels, and the fruit is larger and better flavored than elsewhere. In Sicily, the orange matures the last of October, but here the trees were full of fruit, and much of it green, the first of December.

PLAINS OF SHARON.

The plains of Sharon extend from the Mediterranean Sea, to the mountains of Judah, being about eighteen miles in width, and eighty in length. These plains are spoken of in the Bible as being the most fertile portion of the Promised Land, for the possession of which the Israelites and Philistines fought many a bloody battle. A large portion of this plain is fertile, and when properly cultivated produces large crops, but it is mostly

occupied by Arabs who are indolent, and show but
little skill in agriculture. No forest trees, fencing, nor
farm houses are seen on this plain, but one continuous
open waste, [covered at the time of our visit] with dry
grass and stubble, with here and there an Arab village
surrounded by orange and fig trees.

No rain falls in this country between March and
November, consequently during the summer months,
vegetation dries up, but becomes green again in the
winter. The November rains having started grass and
flowers caused the country in some places to look like
early spring. Along the road in places, the ground was
covered with tulips and lilies, which will bloom in
January, making these plains look at that time like
a vast flower garden. We rode some distance out
of our way, to see the mammoth plant called the rose of
Sharon, supposed to be the flowers so often referred to in
the songs of Solomon. It blooms in February, and the
flower is said to be very large, and of great beauty.

While traveling across these plains, we met an old
Arab with a long, flowing, gray beard, and wearing a
gown made of camel's hair, with a leather girdle around
his loins. He was leading a camel that looked almost as
ancient as himself, on the back of which were four
goat skins filled with water taken out of the river Jordan.
This water was intended for shipment to Europe, for
baptismal purposes.

Farther on we overtook a number of camels packing
goods and lumber from Joppa to Hebron, some of which
were loaded with boards sixteen feet long. On the

back of one of these camels were two barrels of American kerosene oil, marked J. W. Simpson, Center Wells, Pennsylvania. In company with this caravan of packing camels, were a number of women riding donkeys. These women had come from Prussia, and were pilgrims intending to visit the holy places in Palestine. They had already adopted the Oriental style of dress, being covered up with long black robes, and riding astride on their donkeys.

THE ROAD TO JERUSALEM.

Procuring horses at Joppa, we left that city in the afternoon for Jerusalem, which is thirty-eight miles distant. Two miles from Joppa we reached the old city of Lydda, where Peter sojourned for some time, and performed miracles. Ten miles farther on, we came to Ramleh, where we stopped all night at the Latin Convent. Ramleh is a large town, but has a dilapidated appearance with its ruined walls and watch towers, which were built by the crusaders, nine hundred years ago. In the suburbs of the town are many large thickets of cactus twenty feet or more in hight, and full of prickley pears, some of which were ripe and others green.

Along this road are many watch towers, which were built by an appropriation from different governments of Europe, and at one time were occupied by Turkish soldiers to protect the road from robbers, so that pilgrims could pass with safety, to and from Jerusalem.
F*

At different places on the way, we passed large companies of men and women at work on the great carriage road now being constructed by the government between Joppa and Jerusalem. By these workmen, no shovels, wheel-barrows, or carts are used; the dirt being carried in baskets, placed on women's heads. And the stone for building culverts, and macadamizing the road, is brought from the mountain on the backs of camels.

After traveling twenty-two miles on the plains of Sharon, we came to the mountains of Judah, and found the road across them very good, but the country is rocky, barren, and desolate, without forest, grass, or verdure of any kind at this season of the year, except here and there an olive orchard, or a few scattering fig trees.

The people here live in villages, and are engaged in a pastoral life; men are seen herding their flocks of sheep and goats, while women are passing to and fro, carrying water from a neighboring pool or well, in earthen jars placed on their heads, the same as they did two thousand years ago.

In a deep gorge of the mountain called robber's glen, the place was pointed out where thirty years ago the governor of Jerusalem and his guard were killed by a band of robbers headed by their chieftian, Abou Gaush. This band of robbers infested the mountains for many years, setting law at defiance, and levying tribute on travelers. At last the band was broken up, and their chief executed.

Two miles from Jerusalem, we met the Governor of Palestine with his guard of mounted dragoons, and a large retinue of high dignitaries of church and state, all of whom raised their hats to us, and we returned the compliment.

We had become very impatient to obtain a glimpse of the Holy City, but as we reached the summit of a hill, we found one still higher beyond it. At last Jerusalem with its massive walls, and high domes came in sight, which created in me an enthusiasm that I never had felt before, on approaching a strange city. Some of our American friends became so enthusiastic, that they put their horses on a gallop, and rode up to the gate of the city, swinging their hats, and hallooing like rowdies at a political meeting. A telegram from Joppa having reached Jerusalem the evening before, that a party of English and Americans were on the road, caused us to be met outside of the city walls by a number of our own countrymen, who expected to find among us, some of their friends, but were doomed to disappointment.

On entering the city at the Joppa Gate, we were stopped by custom house officers, demanding an examination of baggage, but our baggage having already passed through the custom house at Joppa, was not liable to inspection here. This, the officers well knew, but they contended for backsheesh, claiming two shillings for each valise, which we refused to pay. Further on, we were again stopped by officers demanding passports, which we produced. Our dragoman told us to let the officers read them, but not give them up, as it would cost us

money and much trouble to get them back again.
Taking his advice, we held our passports while the
officers continued to pull on them, ordering us to let go,
but having met with cases like this before, we gave no
heed to their demands. Here we remained for some
time, the officers holding our passports, as well as our
horse's heads, while our dragoman flourished his cane
over their heads, calling them thieves and robbers for
detaining us without authority. At last they offered to
let us go on the payment of five shillings each; this we
refused to do, but told them if further detained, we
would appeal to the British Consul for redress against
this outrage. At this threat they loosed our horses and
passports, and we continued our way into the city.

CHAPTER XXI.

The city of Jerusalem is located on the eastern slope of the mountains of Judah, thirty-eight miles from the Mediterranean, and fourteen from the Dead Sea, and at an elevation of nearly four thousand feet above the latter. It stands on four hills known as follows : Mt. Zion, Mt. Moriah, Akra, and Bezetha. The former two are in the south part, and the latter two in the north part of the city. On the east side of the city, and close under its walls, is the valley of Jehosaphat, and on the west side is the valley of Gehenna. At the junction of these two valleys, which is about a half mile from the city, the ground is over five hundred feet below its common level. South of the city walls, and between these valleys is a piece of table-land covered with stone and rubbish from ruined buildings, and decayed walls. North of the city, is another piece of land covered over in a like manner, showing that both of these tracts at one time were within the walls, and constituted a part of the city.

Jerusalem is surrounded by walls two and a half miles in length, fifteen feet thick, and from forty to seventy feet high. The top of these walls are ornamented with cornice work, and guarded on either side by terrace walls, so that a person can walk on them, entirely around the city. A short distance apart are towers mounted with cannon, and containing quarters for soldiers. Through the walls of these towers are port holes, so the guards can fire on the enemy in time of war.

There are five gates through the walls, named as follows: Joppa, Damascus, St. Stephen, Mt. Zion, and Dirty Gate, the latter being used only for carrying out filth of the city. Beside these five is the Golden Gate on Mt. Moriah, which is now walled up. The walls at these gates are high and thick, and the passage through them turns in the center, so that things on the inside cannot be seen. During the day time these gates are guarded by soldiers, but at dark their great iron shutters are locked, which cuts off all communication between the city and country.

From the summit of Mt. Olivet, Jerusalem has quite an imposing appearance with its high walls running zigzag in various directions, and ornamented at the top with cornice work. Its many mosques with high domes and countless minarets, and houses having dome roofs, all built of white stone, will remind a person of the description given of it in the day of Josephus. But upon entering the city, all its pomp and grandeur is lost, and a person is apt to reconsider his first impressions. Its streets are dark, dirty alleys, crowded with filthy

looking Arabs, camels, donkeys, and dogs, while offensive smells rising from various kinds of nuisances, fill
the nasal organs at every turn. The streets do not
exceed ten feet in width, and are paved with rough
stone; many of them are arched over at the top with
houses built thereon, which form long, dark arcades,
where the light of day is admitted through openings
in the walls, at long intervals. In these dark caverns,
people live, have stores or shops of trade, and transact
business, the same as in other streets of the city.

The buildings are mostly three stories high, constructed entirely of stone, except doors and windows,
having stone floors, and stone arched ceiling in each
room. Many of the houses are without window glass,
its place being supplied by iron bars. Some of the
houses have domes on their top, others are flat, and used
for flower gardens, goat yards, play grounds for children,
a place for drying clothes, and frequently containing a
praying post, by the side of which the head of the family
goes night and morning to pray. The lower stories
are mostly used for stores, shops, or stabling for donkeys
and camels, while the families live up stairs. There is
no gas used here, and all business places close at dark,
when stillness and gloom reigns throughout the city.
But few people are seen on the streets after dark, as
the police are authorized to arrest any one found at
night unless carrying a lantern. Water to supply the
city is carried through the streets in goat skins on the
backs of donkeys or camels, and sold to the occupants
of each house. Stone, lumber, mortar, and all kinds

of produce, merchandize, etc., are carried in a like manner.

No wagon or carriage had ever been seen within the walls of Jerusalem, until a short time since Mr. Floyd, the Yankee hackman drove his carriage through Joppa gate, and along the street as far as the Mediterranean hotel to the great astonishment of the people, most of whom had never seen any thing on wheels before. Large crowds of people followed the carriage, blocking up the street, and the trouble he had in turning around, and getting out again, discouraged him from making a like attempt again.

The population of Jerusalem is estimated at twenty-five thousand, but varies at different periods, according to the number of Christian and Jewish pilgrims sojourning here. The Christian population is said to number four thousand, the greater portion of whom are converted Arabs, being nominally Christians for a pecuniary consideration, inasmuch as they recieve part of their support from the Mt. Zion Mission.

The accompanying view of Jerusalem is taken from the south-west, on the Hill of Evil Council, and does not show its beautiful walls. To the right is seen the Mosque of Omar on Mt. Moriah. To the left on the southern slope of Mt. Zion is to be seen the Turkish mosque covering the tomb of David, as well as the buildings around the pool of Hezekiah. The large dome seen in the background is on the church of the Holy Sepulchre.

VIEW OF JERUSALEM FROM THE HILL OF EVIL COUNSEL.

as fear of contagion. Outside of their quarters, they will not approach near any one, but keep themselves at a respectful distance. The disease preys on all parts of the body, and makes its appearance in various forms; some with red swollen faces and limbs, the hair of their heads, beard, and eyebrows, having fallen off; others with their chin or nose eaten off, and many of their fingers and toes missing. The leprosy is hereditary, and those afflcted with it, intermarry, thus entailing this dreadful disease on their posterity. I saw young babes with this disease, the skin almost black, and covered over with running sores, being a mass of corruption. With other chidren who were almost grown the disease had not yet made its appearance. Persons who have drawn their ideas of this horrible disease from the Bible account, will have a strange sensation when coming in contact with these lepers.

Outside of the Joppa and Mt. Zion gates, many of these lepers are seen sitting on the ground from morning until night, begging alms from those passing by. Their distorted faces, swollen limbs, and hairless heads, together with their piteous wailings, are sickening to behold.

TRADITIONARY PLACES IN JERUSALEM.

Jerusalem is full of traditionary places, almost every place spoken of in the Bible being now pointed out to a stranger. Many of these places are purely imaginary while in others, everybody appear to have full confidence as to their genuineness. During my fifteen days stay in Jerusalem, I visited almost every place of interest, not only in the city, but in its surroundings, and seeing the permanent manner in which these buildings were constructed has changed my mind with regard to them. Instead of being skeptical on this point, I became a believer in the genuineness of many of these traditionary places.

In the south part of Jerusalem is located Mt. Zion, much celebrated in all ages of Jewish history; on it stood the palace of David and Solomon, as well as other kings of Judah. On its southern slope is the tomb of David, over which is built a mosque, now guarded by Turkish soldiers. On the summit of Mt. Zion, stands the Tower of David, consisting of a massive stone structure fifty-five feet high, and mounted with cannon. Near this is pointed out the palace of Caiaphas, the high priest, where the scribes and elders met to take council against Christ.

North of Mt. Zion there is a slight eminence, known as Mt. Calvary, on which is located the church of the Holy Sepulchre, originally built by order of Empress Helena, in A. D. 326. This church is said to occupy the place where Christ was crucified and entombed, and contains many things relating to that event. The church is a very large one, and contains three chapels, one each for the Latins, Greek, and Armenians. In the center of the building is a large rotunda capped by a beautiful dome. In one part of the church is the Holy Sepulchre, purporting to be the place where Christ was laid. This consists of a room, eight feet square, cut out of the native rock, and cased with white marble. Around the entrance of this vault are forty-two silver and gold lamps, which are kept burning day and night. At all hours of the day, people are seen kneeling before the Holy Sepulchre, and kissing the rock of Divine Unction, while their loud weeping and wailings, frequently bring tears to the eyes of the bystanders. There are many things here relating to Christ's crucifixion, such as a part of the veil of the temple, two large rocks which were rent, also the rock with a hole in it, on which the cross was erected.

Being provided with lights, and conducted by a guide, we examined the basement of this church which is carved out of a solid rock, and in which we saw many of the wonderful things of Mt. Calvary. Through the different parts of the church, as well as outside of its walls, are stationed Turkish soldiers to guard these sacred places, and to prevent the Christian pilgrims cutting each others' throats.

In the east part of the city, near Mt. Moriah, is located the palace of Pilate, consisting of a large, ancient looking edifice, which is now occupied by officers connected with the government. On the outside of this building are still to be seen marks in the wall, where stairs had evidently been taken out. Here, said our dragoman, is where once stood the holy stairs which Christ ascended to the judgment seat of Pilate. I had seen these holy stairs at Rome, in the church of St. John Laterena, and counted the steps, which correspond with the marks in the wall, being twenty-eight each. From the palace of

Pilate to Mt. Calvary, is nearly a half mile, and the street connecting these points is called the Sorrowful Way, along which Christ is said to have passed, bearing his cross to the place of crucifixion. Processions are sometimes formed by priests, monks, and pilgrims, to march from the palace of Pilate to Calvary, along the Sorrowful Way, and their cries and lamentations can be heard above all other noise of the city.

Near the harem, on Mt. Moriah, is still to be seen the pool of Bethesda, and also the celebrated tower of Antonio, both of which are now in a state of ruins.

On the west side of the temple walls, can be seen the remains of a bridge across the Tyropean valley, which connected Mt. Zion with Mt. Moriah. This bridge according to Josephus, was built by Solomon, and over it, he passed in going back and forth to worship in the temple, and in all probability it was one of the great works of Israel's king that astonished the Queen of Sheba. There are five arches in this bridge, each of which is forty-one feet in width, but only a part of one of these is above ground, and this is constructed of large stone, twenty feet long, by six feet thick. Within the last year, Lieutenant Warren, of the English Excavating Company, has sunk a number of shafts here, which show the foundation of the bridge, as well as the original ground in the valley to be sixty feet below the present level of the street.

MOUNT MORIAH.

In the east part of Jerusalem, between Mt. Zion, and the

mount of Olives, is located Mt. Moriah, on which once
stood the temple of Solomon. This place is called the
harem (a sacred place), being surrounded by an inner
wall, and the gate leading therein is guarded by soldiers,
and no one but Mohammedans is allowed to enter it
without a pass. For more than six hundred years, Mt.
Moriah was secluded from both Christians and Jews, and
any one found therein forfeited his life, as the guards were
authorized to slay all infidels found in this sacred place.
But of late years this principle of intolerance has been
modified so that strangers are admitted by having a
pass from the Governor of Jerusalem, when they are
accompanied by a file of soldiers, and everything of
interest pointed out.

Mt. Moriah is the lowest of the four hills on which
Jerusalem is built. Between it and Mt. Zion lies the
Tyropean valley, once a deep ravine with rocky sides.
But with the ruins of the ancient city, as well as the
washing of many centuries, this valley is now almost
filled up to the common level of the city. Near the
south-west corner of the wall which surrounds Mt.
Moriah, is the place of wailing. Here the wall is constructed of large stone of twenty feet or more in length
and is said to have been put there by Solomon. By this
wall we found a number of Jews praying, weeping, and
wailing over what they called the only relic of the
ancient temple. These Jews had come here as pilgrims
from foreign countries. One of whom was an old man
with a long, white beard, with tears running down his
furrowed cheeks. He said that he was a Jewish Rabbi,

and lived in England, having traveled a distance of four thousand miles to see the Holy City, and was denied the privilege of visiting the site of the temple a place regarded by Jews as the most sacred spot on earth.

Being provided with the necessary papers, and accompanied by a file of solders, as well as our dragoman, we had an opportunity of seeing Mt. Moriah, and walking over the ground once trod by Abraham, David and Solomon, and also by Christ, and the Apostles. There are about thirty acres enclosed within the walls, containing many paved walks and small flower plats, with a few cypress trees, and other shrubbery. Near the center of the enclosure is the mosque of Omar, occupying the site of the ancient temple. This building stands on a marble base elevated above the level of the ground, and is nearly round, with a large dome in the center. Mohammedans regard this mosque, after their parent one at Mecca the finest in the world, but to me it appears more showy than grand. In passing through it, we were provided with slippers so that our boots might not defile the holy place.* Here within the walls of the harem are many other mosques and public buildings, some of which are used as institutions of learning, and all show signs of great antiquity. Close to the Mosque of Omar is the sacred rock, rising ten or twelve feet above ground, and about fifty feet square, and showing no marks of the chisel or hammer as far as I could see. It is surrounded by an iron gilt railing

---

* For a view of this mosque see frontispiece.

and covered by a silk awning, being regarded the most sacred spot in the harem.

Tradition locates many of the great events narrated in the Bible as having occured on this rock, all of which were explained to us by our dragoman. As Abraham came journeying from Beersheba with his son Isaac, he ascended Mt. Moriah, and on this rock offered him up as a sacrifice, when his hand was stayed by an angel. Many centuries afterwards, Ornan the Jebusite occupied the base of this rock as a threshing floor, when the avenging angel appeared sword in hand threatening the destruction of the Holy City, and scaring away Ornan and his four sons. David having seen the angel from the hight of Mt. Zion, and to avert the threatening evil, bought the threshing floor of Ornan for six hundred shekles of gold, and built an altar thereon. It was on this rock, fronting the temple, that sacrifices were offered up in all ages of Judaism, from the days of David to the destruction of Jerusalem by the Roman army. These, and many other things relating to Bible history the dragoman explained to us, after which he gave us a few passages from the Koran, relating to Mohammedan faith.

When Mohammed made his celebrated tour from Mecca to Jerusalem, and thence through the heavens, he ascended from this rock. Here was pointed out to us the prints of his feet, also the the marks of the angels hands, made by holding the rock down so as to prevent it from taking an aerial voyage with the prophet, and many other miraculous things relating to Mohammed.

H*

At this statement one of our party stopped the dragoman in his eloquent narration, by telling him that he did not wish to hear any more on that subject, as the feet and hand marks were too much for him to believe. At these remarks the dragoman grew angry, saying that such infidels as we were, never should have been allowed to enter the harem, and walk over these sacred grounds.

Under the ground are found many vaulted chambers with long colonades running in various directions, which constituted a part of the temple. At one place there is a pool of water, said to be the fountain which supplies that of the Virgin, and pool of Siloam. In different parts of the enclosure, shafts have been sunk by the English Excavating Company, showing in some places the foundation of the temple to be sixty or seventy feet under ground. I have talked with Jews living at Jerusalem, who believe that the ark of the covenant, the mercy seat, and cherubims, all made of solid gold now lie hidden in some of these vaults under the temple, and at some future day they will be found and restored to Israel. Close to the mosque of Omar, is the golden gate, passing through the outer wall in the direction of Bethany. Through this gate, Christ is said to have passed when he made his grand entry into Jerusalem. It is now walled up, and no use made of it. At this point we ascended the wall, which is here, thirty feet high on the inside and seventy feet on the outside, overlooking the valley of Jehoshaphat which lies almost under it, and beyond, which is the mount of Olives.

While walking over Mt. Moriah, many of the great

events which transpired here, were brought fresh to my mind, and I found myself lost in meditation. On this spot the Jews made their last defence against the army of Titus. Having taken refuge within the temple walls, it being their last stronghold, here they were overpowered and slain by thousands. Many centuries afterwards the crusaders beseiged the Moslem hordes entrenched on this ground, when the same barbarous excesses were again enacted, and twelve thousand Mohammedans were slain. History says this area at the time of the slaughter was ankle deep in blood.

CHAPTER XXII.

After spending some days in seeing sights within the walls of Jerusalem, we made a number of excursions in its vicinity. Passing out at the gate of St. Stephen we came to the place where tradition says the Apostle was stoned to death. From here we crossed the valley of Jehoshaphat, and visited the garden of Gethsemane, which is situated on the western slope of the mount of Olives. This garden consists of a small piece of ground not exceeding one acre, enclosed by a high stone wall, and guarded by a monk, who admitted us when we rang the bell at the gate. Here in the garden are many flower beds, between which are paved walks, bordered by box, and other ornamental shrubs. Within the walls of the garden are eight old olive trees, the largest of which I measured, and found to be nineteen feet in circumference. The monk pointed out to us many places connected with the acts of Christ and the Apostles, not forgetting to show us the spot where Judas stood when he received the thirty pieces of silver. I gave the monk in attendance two shillings for his kind attention to us, and in return he picked for me a beautiful bouquet of Oriental flowers, part of which I brought home as a memento.

From the garden of Gethsemane, we ascended the mount of Olives, which is the highest point around Jerusalem, and from its summit the whole country for miles can be seen. Here on the summit is a small Arab village containing a Turkish mosque, and also a small Latin chapel called the Church of Ascension. Of the tall cedars covering the summit of this mountain, and the beautiful palms along its slope, described by Josephus, not one is now to be seen. A few olive and fig trees, with here and there a small piece of cultivated land, between piles of stone and bowlders are all that is now seen on this desolate mountain.

On the southern slope of the mount of Olives are the tombs of the prophets, consisting of catacombs cut out of the rock which can be explored by the assistance of a guide carrying lights. Close by these tombs, tradition points out the place of Christ's ascension.

On the east side of the valley of Jehoshaphat, stands Absalom's pillar, or tomb, which consists of a large open base or pedestal, and from which rises a shaft ornamented with columns and pilasters, fifty-two feet high. People passing this tomb throw stones in at the windows, out of contempt for the rebellious son of David, until a large pile of stone and rubbish has accumulated many feet in hight. Near Absalom's Pillar, is the tomb of

Zechariah, cut in a solid rock and a monument built
thereon. Here, too, is the tomb of Jehoshaphat, having
a large doorway, highly ornamented with carved work,
and showing much beauty in its construction. Most all
writers on the antiquities of Palestine, believe these
tombs to be genuine, and built at the time they purport
to have been.

From these ancient tombs we followed down the valley of Jehoshaphat, along the brook Kedron, (which is
dry except during the winter rains,) until we came to the
village of Siloam. This village consists of a few houses
built on a rocky cliff, and has a very ancient appearance.
Opposite the village, is to be seen the pool of Siloam,
which has been so often referred to in the Bible, as
a place where miracles were wrought. In descending
to this pool, we went down a flight of sixteen stone steps
to a wide stone platform, and from here is another
flight of steps descending to the water. The water in
the pool is a running stream of about fifteen inches
depth, from which is a large tunnel conveying to
other places. On the upper side of the pool, there
is a tunnel about six feet wide, and eight feet high,
cut out of native rock, through which the water flows
from the Fountain of the Virgin, three hundred feet
above. Women from the village were here after water,
and would go down into it with their feet, while they
filled their jars and goat skins, the same as they did at
the time of Christ.

The road leading from the gate of St. Stephen to the
garden of Gethsemane crosses the brook Kedron on a

stone bridge of some twenty feet in hight. After crossing this bridge we came to the chapel and tomb of the
Virgin Mary, which is situated on the western slope of
Mt. Olivet. The chapel is partly below the common
level of the ground, its foundation being excavated out
of the native rock, and has an ancient appearance.
On entering the chapel, we descended a flight of sixty
stone steps, through a dark, gloomy looking passage-
way. The inside of the chapel is decorated in a gaudy
manner, and on the wall are many large paintings illustrating scenes in the life of the Virgin. From the
ceiling are suspended fifty-six gold and silver lamps
which are kept continually burning. The gloom and
solemnity of the chapel was increased by the light
of these lamps as it is reflected from glass shades of
various colors.

On one side of the church is a grotto, cut out of the
rock, highly ornamented and lighted with lamps. Connected with this grotto is the tomb in which the Virgin
Mary is said to have been laid, and near it is the tomb
of Joseph, her husband.

On the south-west side of the city, and almost under
its walls, is the valley of Gehenna, or Tophet of the
Bible, where in ancient times all the filth of the city
was thrown, as well as the remains of persons executed
for crime, and also children sacrificed to the god of
Moloch, until God by the prophets pronounced a curse
against the valley. To day this valley is used in part
for the same purpose. Above it is the dirty gate,
through which the filth of the city is carried to be

thrown into the valley. While passing along here, I found the smell rising from decayed matter, and dead animals almost unendurable. South of this valley is the Hill of Evil Council, and beyond it, is the Potters' field, or Golgotha of Scripture, covered over with tombs and catacombs. On the opposite side of the valley is the Mt. of Corruption, where one of the wicked kings built a temple to the god of Moloch, the remains of which were pointed out by our guide.

At the junction of the brook Kedron and Gihon, is that part of the valley called Hinnom, sometimes termed the Universalists' hell. Near this is the king's gardens, as well as other places referred to in the Bible. Here in this valley, five hundred feet below the city, is still to be seen Joab's well, spoken of in the days of King David, and also at different periods of the Jewish history. This well is very large, walled with heavy cut stone, and arched over at the top, and the water is drawn from it with leather buckets or jars attached to a rope as in ancient times. Many deep creases are worn in the wall by the rope going up and down for many centuries.

West of the city and in the valley of Gehenna, are the ruins of two pools, called the upper and lower pool of Gihon, said to have been built nearly twenty-five hundred years ago. These pools were constructed by building high stone walls across the valley, so as to dam the water which flows in it during the rainy season, and thereby retaining a supply for all the year. Between these pools are still to be seen the remains of an arched aqueduct across the valley, which at one time conveyed water from the pools of Solomon, near Bethlehem, to the temple on Mt. Moriah.

North of the city are the tombs of the Judges, and close by them are the tombs of the Kings. These tombs consist of catacombs, or large chambers cut out of the rocks, and can be explored by employing guides carrying lights. I had spent much time in Italy rambling through the dark vaulted chambers of the dead, and had no desire to visit these. Under the city is a large cavern made by taking out stone for building purposes. This cavern is said to contain many strange things, but I cannot vouch for the truth of these statements.

Jerusalem has no suburbs, and around it are rocky barren hills, without trees, dwellings, or farming land. But within the last few years the Emperor of Russia has built on the west side of the city walls, a fine Greek church, with other buildings, forming quite a colony. About a half mile from this colony, on the opposite side of the valley of Gehenna, a wealthy Jew has built a number of houses, terraced the land, planted vineyards, and fig trees, restoring it again to its former fertility, which is in strange contrast to the barreness and desolation surrounding it.

PALESTINE AS IT NOW APPEARS.

In traveling through the lands of Ephraim, Dan, Benjamin, and Judah, I found much of the country wild, barren and desolate, consisting of mountains of rocks and

I*

plains of sand.   In many places where cities are located
on the ancient map of Palestine, nothing now remains
but piles of stone from ruined walls, and decayed
buildings.   Along the slope of the mountains are still to
be seen the remains of walls where the land had been
terraced, and where the grape and fig were cultivated;
but now it is an open common, a pasture for sheep and
goats.   In places where streams are laid down on maps,
I find in most cases a dry, rocky hollow, where water
runs only during the winter rains.   The water to supply
the country is found in wells or pools.   The pools are
mostly sunk deep into the ground, arched over at the
top, and the water in them is reached by long flights of
stone steps.   The country is without timber, coal, or
peat, and the fuel mostly in use here, consists of roots
from a shrub that grows on the mountains.

Palestine according to history was at one time a very
productive country, supporting a large population; but
to day a great portion of it is uninhabited, a barren
waste, where the roving bedouins pitch their tents, and
the hyena, and wild boar are undisturbed by human
habitation.   Who knows whether these changes are the
the result of natural causes, or a judgment of the
Almighty, in the fulfillment of the prophecy which
says, "Its cities shall be leveled, and its highways made
desolate."

Farm houses are not seen in the country, and all the
inhabitants live in villages, so as to protect each other
from bands of robbers, who are all the while roaming
through the country.   People on the mountains are

principally engaged in a pastoral life, raising sheep and goats, which are herded on the mountains at all seasons of the year. The goats of Palestine are mostly black, and the sheep are generally of the same color, some of which are of the Lebanon breed, with large flat tails. The inhabitants of the plains are engaged in cultivating the soil, where they raise various kinds of grain, such as wheat, corn, and rice, besides sugar cane. Wheat is sown in the Fall and harvested in March or April. Grass is green during the winter months, which is the rainy season, but it is burnt out in the summer, as no rain falls here between March and November.

On the mountains of Judah, which are elevated nearly three thousand feet above the sea, the atmosphere is bracing, and snow sometimes falls, but in the valleys it is always warm. In traveling on the plains in December, we found the heat oppressive, making it necessary to carry umbrellas over our heads to shield us from the scorching rays of the sun. A large portion of the inhabitants of the plains, both male and female, dress themselves in blue cotton gowns, and go barefooted at all seasons of the year.

During my stay in Palestine and Egypt, I never saw a cloud in the sky, the atmosphere being always clear, with the sun shining in all its brilliancy.

In Jerusalem there are two hotels, the Mediterranean and Damascus, which are kept by Europeans, but hotels are not found in other parts of Palestine, and a person traveling through the country is obliged to camp out. In some of the larger towns are found a Greek or Latin monastery, where the tourist can find lodging. East of the mountains of Judah, and along the Dead Sea and the Jordan, the country is full of Bedouins, or robbers, and to visit these localities it is necessary to be accompanied by a guard of soldiers.

EXCURSION TO JERICHO, AND DEAD SEA.

We had provided ourselves with a dragoman, tents and a guard of Turkish soldiers, for a three days tour in the plains of Jericho. But at Bethlehem I was taken sick and returned, while the party continued on their journey without me. Feeling better the next day, I procured the services of a dragoman with good horses, and by sunrise we were on the road galloping over the mountains in the direction of Jericho. Two miles from Jerusalem we came to Bethany, a village of some twenty houses, and partly surrounded by olive trees. Here we stopped to see the house of Mary and Martha, as well as that of Simon, the leper. We also visited the tomb of Lazarus which consists of a deep, dark vault, cut out of solid rock, and reached by a long flight of stone steps. My faith in these traditions is not very strong, so we mounted our horses and were again on the road. Our way was over a wild looking country, along a rocky path, under leaning rocks, and by the side of frightful precipices. While on our way, I thought of the man spoken of in Scripture, who in traveling this road, eighteen hundred years ago, fell among thieves, and I was fearful of meeting the same fate myself.

In one of the rocky defiles, we saw two Arabs at work with hammers and picks, cutting away the rock, so as to procure the honey of wild bees, which is said to be plenty among these cliffs. The dragoman said to me while on the road, that we were close to Elijah's cave, and by going a mile or two out of our way, he would show me the place where the prophet was miraculously fed by the ravens. But having already seen so many remarkable things at Bethany, I had become quite skeptical in regard to these old traditions, and declined going.

After two hours ride, we came to a point which overlooked the plains of Jericho, and here was pointed out the location of the three Jerichos, spoken of in history. No remains of either of these ancient cities could be seen from where we stood, but I understand that ruins of two of them can be seen among the sand drifts. The present city of Jericho is only a cluster of Arab huts, and its inhabitants are said to be thieves and cut-throats, the same as they were at the time of Christ.

The plain of Jericho is about ten miles wide, and was once noted for its fertility, being called the land of palms, but is now a barren waste, covered over with drifting sand. This plain is almost without trees, shrubs, or grass, except a small green spot around the miserable city of Jericho, and over it roams undisturbed the hyena and jackall. Through this plain flows the river Jordan, but from where we stood, I could not see its waters, though its windings were visible among the willows. We could see the mouth of the river Arnon, as it mixed with that of the Jordan, at the head of North Bay. Far beyond the Jordan, were seen the blue outlines of Mt. Pisgah, from whose summit the Israelites viewed the Promised Land.

Leaving Jericho, we traveled southward along the eastern slope of the mountain, until we came close to the Dead Sea, and from this point, all of its surface was visible. This sea is said to be forty miles long, and ten miles wide, but in the clear atmosphere which surrounds it, a person would think it less than half that size. Down in a deep valley, thirteen hundred feet below the ocean, lies this large body of torpid water, looking clear and blue, but so impregnated with saline matter, that no living thing is found therein. No sails are seen on its surface, nor trees, verdure, nor habitation along its shores, but stillness, loneliness, and gloom reign supreme, and well may it be termed the sea of death. Beyond the Dead Sea, were seen the barren, rocky mountains of Moab, the land of the ancient Moabites, among whom tourists seldom venture.

From where we stood, the D ead Sea appeared almost under us, and I tried to prevail on the dragoman to go with me to its shores, so that I might bathe in its waters, But he refused to go saying that I would be in danger of falling into the hands of Bedouins, who frequently roam through this country.

I had heard much about the apples of Sodom, and felt a great desire to see some of them. Knowing that this fruit is only found in the vicinity of the Dead Sea, I offered the dragoman additional pay if he would show me some of them. In our search we followed down a dry wady, until we came to a plain of sand and rock, almost at the edge of the sea. The prospect of the extra shilling, which I had promised the dragoman caused him to forget all about the danger of Bedouins and we were now as he afterward expressed himself on dangerous ground. Among the rocks and sand, we found a small cluster of trees which resembled stunted haw-thorn, and on these were growing the celebrated apple of Sodom. I must confess that I was much disappointed in the appearance of the fruit, as I had expected to find large highly colored apples, inviting to the taste. But instead of these, were seen hanging here and there on the trees, small, green looking fruit, about the size of a Romanite. The fruit had not yet fully matured, some of which appeared to be not more than half grown. I cut open a number of these apples, and found them to be porous, and extremely bitter. I am informed when fully ripe they are of a yellow color, and by pressing them in the hand, will dissolve in smoke and dust like a puff ball.

While among these rocky defiles, another fruit-bearing shrub was pointed out, which is called carob, or locust. This fruit grows in a pod resembling the coffee nut. In some parts of Palestine it is said to grow in great abundance, and is used by the natives as an article of diet. This fruit is thought to be the same spoken of in Scripture. John the Baptist is said to have lived on locusts and wild honey, both of which are now found here in the wilderness of Judea.

From the Dead Sea, we shaped our course homeward and arrived in Jerusalem at sundown, after a ride of more than forty miles over a mountainous country.

CHAPTER XXIII.

Bethlehem is six miles south of Jerusalem, and the road leading thereto runs part of the way along the slope of the mountain, then through the plains of Rephaim. Although this road has been traveled for more than three thousand years, and is one of the principal highways of Palestine, it shows no sign of ever having been worked, and over it no wagon or carriage has ever passed. Along it, the scenery is wild and desolate, without farms, or farm houses, but here and there are seen large piles of stone, the remains of ruined castles, or watch towers. Two miles from Jerusalem, we entered the plains of Rephaim, on which David fought two battles with the Philistines. In the middle of the road, on these plains is the well of Rebecca, or Maji, memorable for many events narrated in the Bible. Around this well are many stone troughs for watering horses or camels, and near it are the remains of ruined buildings. South of the Maji well on high ground, overlooking both Jerusalem

J*

and Bethlehem, is located the Greek Convent of St. Elias, or Elijah. This convent is surrounded by a high stone wall, giving to it a fort like appearance, and is said to occupy the spot where Elijah rested, when fleeing from his persecutors.

To the right of the road on high ground, one mile from Bethlehem, is Rachel's tomb. Consisting of a massive stone structure, built like a Turkish mosque, and ornamented by a dome. The Bible says as Jacob and his family were traveling from Bethel to Hebron, Rachel fell sick, died, and was buried near Bethlehem by the wayside, and a pillar was erected over her grave.

Having parted with my company at Bethlehem, and returning to Jerusalem along this road, I met with an adventure which was both exciting and mysterious. While riding slowly along the rocky road, two Arabs mounted on fine horses, and carrying in their hands, long spears of polished steel, came out of a gorge of the mountain, into the road. These men placed themselves in the road before me, and commenced conversation, but I could understand nothing they said, but backsheesh. To their earnest appeals, I only shook my head, which caused them to be more bold in their demands for money. For some way they continued in my company, occasionally stopping before me, directly in the path. At last they rode on ahead for some ways, then turning back they came towards me on a full gallop, with their spears drawn in a threatening attitude, and passed by me, one on either side. Here they stopped and conversed with each other for a moment, then turned their horses and galloped off in a different direction.

When I arrived at my hotel in Jerusalem, I related this strange adventure, and people expressed different opinions with regard to it. Some thought these men were government rangers, and only wished to show their good horsemanship, while others believed them to have been Bedouins, and not succeeding in frightening me so as to give them money, left again for their old range. These Bedouins are sometimes seen on the mountains, and even around the walls of Jerusalem, but were never known to commit robberies here, as they are afraid of the Turkish soldiers. But on the plains of Jericho, they rob every person not under government protection, sometimes taking all their clothes, and turning them adrift in a state of nudity.

BETHLEHEM.

With the exception of Jerusalem, no city of Palestine is so much visited by tourists as Bethlehem. Here Abraham pitched his tent, and here David was born, and on its mountain slopes he herded his sheep. It was here Joseph and Mary found a resting place, and where Christ made his advent into the world. Bethlehem is said to contain a population of four thousand, a large portion of whom profess to be Christians. The city is built on a hillside, with one street rising above another which gives to it a formidable appearance. The houses are built of gray stone, flat on the top, and many of their massive walls are cracked, giving to them a dilapidated appearance. ' The entrance from the north is through a high arched gateway, being a relic of the high wall which once surrounded the city.

As we rode through the streets of Bethlehem, men and women came out of their houses and shops to look at us, and a large crowd of boys followed us to hold our horses, or render any service for which they could claim backsheesh. A large portion of the traffic is carried on in the streets, or open squares, and the appearance of the people engaged in trade, is in keeping with the scene of poverty and desolation which surrounds them. Here were old men sitting on the ground with a pile of wheat before them spread out on a cloth, and selling it by the quart. Here too, were women seated on mother earth, selling trinkets and calling on each passerby, with piteous tones, saying, " For the sake of Christ, or of God, and Mohammed, come and buy of me."

On high ground in the east part of the city, is located the Church of the Nativity, said to be built over the cave, or manger where Christ was born. This church, or convent was built by Empress Helena, A. D. 325, and contains two chapels, and a large reception and dining room, to accommodate pilgrims visiting Bethlehem. The building is surrounded by a. massive wall, through which are loop-holes, for placing cannon, to be used in time of war, causing it to look more like a fort than a church or convent.

A monk carrying a lighted candle led us down a long

flight of steps into the basement, showing us the cave, or grotto cut out of the native rock, where Christ was born. Over the entrance of this cave is a marble slab, on which is a large silver star, of some twenty inches in diameter, and around this is engraved in Latin, these words, "Here Jesus Christ was born of Virgin Mary." Around the star and motto are suspended sixteen silver lamps, which are kept continually burning. Here are gold and silver ornaments, as well as large paintings illustrating the advent of Christ.

To the right of the holy grotto is to be seen the altar of innocence consecrated to the babes whom Herod caused to be slain in hope of destroying the infant Christ, and beyond it is the cave where the dead bodies were thrown.

We were shown in this basement the chapel, and studio, of St. Jerome where he spent much of his life. In this dark and gloomy vault, more than fourteen hundred years ago he wrote his celebrated works. Close by the chapel of St. Jerome excavated out of the native rock, and faced with marble, is to be seen his tomb, containing many interesting things which relate to the departed saint.

SURROUNDINGS OF BETHLEHEM.

In the suburbs of Bethlehem are many grottos cut out of the rock, similar to the one under the Church of the Nativity, the traditionary birth place of Christ. These grottos are principally used as stables for

camels and donkeys, but a few of them are occupied as
dwellings for the poorer classes. The land around Bethlehem, unlike Jerusalem, is quite fertile, with cultivated
fields, and orchards of figs and olives. On these fields
are many watch towers, where the guards are quartered
to protect the crops from the depredations of robbers.

It was in one of these fields, Ruth gleaned after the
reapers, and here the sons of Jesse were at work when
the prophet Samuel came to annoint David, King of
Israel.

A short distance from Bethlehem is a narrow valley
covered with fields of grain, and green pastures, among
which is a small Arab village called Etham. The land
in this valley is irrigated by a fountain which flows close
by, and by that means two crops a year are raised
off the same land. Here the grass was green, with
wheat and rice fields almost ready for harvest, while
vegetation in other parts of Palestine was burnt out by
the summer drouth. Within the last few years, excavations have been made in this valley which have brought
to light many interesting things. Among the ruins
discovered, are the remains of a large building, with
a marble floor inlaid with mosaic work, and in the
rear of this, are a number of baths, also constructed of
marble. This place is thought to be the site of ancient
Etham, where Solomon had his gardens and vineyards.

In this valley are the celebrated pools of Solomon,
which have been so much commented upon by writers
upon Palestine. Here are three pools or reservoirs,
averaging about four hundred feet in length, three

hundred feet in width, and forty feet in depth. These pools are partly cut out of the rock, with walls built on the lower side, and coated with cement. They rise one above another, so that the same water flows through all of them. The water to supply these pools comes from a spring some distance above, and enters them by a subterranean passage through the rocks. These pools are always full of water, and from them is an aqueduct which conveys it to Bethlehem, two miles distant.

From the pools of Solomon, there is an old aqueduct now in ruins, which in former times conveyed the water to Jerusalem, six miles distant. This aqueduct is constructed of heavy masonry, and follows the windings of the hill, so as to keep nearly on a level. In some places it is underground, then crossing valleys on arched bridges, and along rocky cliffs, until it reaches the temple wall on Mt. Moriah. We followed the course of this aqueduct in many of its windings, and examined some of its bridges, one of which crosses the valley of Gihon. This bridge is about three hundred feet long, and fifty feet high.

All writers agree that this great work was done by Solomon, as many allusions are made to it in the Bible. Josephus speaks of a place called Etham, six miles from Jerusalem, where Solomon had gardens and vineyards. Here he also built pools and brought the water from them into the temple, on Mt. Moriah.

Leaving Jerusalem early in the morning, we made a visit to the ruins of Mizpeh, which on account of their historical associations, are considered the most interesting in Palestine. While on the road to Mizpeh, and some four miles north-west of Jerusalem we came to the valley of Philistia, in which is situated a small Arab village. Near this village is a piece of table-land partly surrounded by rocky cliffs which is pointed out as the place where David killed Goliah. As we left this valley and while passing through the village, we saw at some distance a woman engaged as we supposed, in hanging a dog. Turning our horses in that direction, to our surprise, we found that she was churning. The cream was in a goat skin which hung by the neck to a limb of an olive tree, on which she had a rope tied, to spring the limb up and down, to produce the butter. The long, black hair of the goat skin, with its legs and tail flopping up and down by the springing of the limb, looked like an animal in the agonies of death. This churn for ease and convenience of working, certainly exceeds all of the new Yankee patents now in use.

Three miles from the valley of Philistia, we came to Mt. Neby, on which once stood the city of Mizpeh, the home and burial place of the prophet Samuel. We visited what is said to be the prophet's tomb, which consists of a vault cut out of the rock, and surrounded at the mouth with heavy masonry. Around this tomb, Christian, Jewish and Mohammedan pilgrims, alike, are seen to weep and pray, and from it the Bible says the witch of Endor caused the dead prophet to come forth.

Here on Mt. Neby, Samuel called Israel together to elect a king, when the choice fell upon Saul. Then for the first time in Israel the multitude shouted "God save the king." Eight hundred years ago, the crusaders built a convent here, the remains of which are still to be seen, and close by it, are the ruins of a Mohammedan mosque. These ruins and large piles of stone lying around among Arab huts are all that now remain to mark the spot where once stood the populous city of Mizpeh.

Mt. Neby is the highest point in this vicinity, and from it a fine view of the country can be obtained, overlooking the plains of Sharon, and the Mediterranean Sea. I had seen much fine scenery among the Alps, but nothing to equal this. The clearness, and transparency of the atmosphere is such that objects twenty or thirty miles off appear close by. From here Remlah, Lydda, Joppa, and other cities of the plain can be seen. Although it was December, the weather was quite warm, and appeared like a bright June day, without wind or clouds.

The name of this mountain does not occur in Scriptures, but frequent allusion is made to the places situated upon it, and deeds which there occurred.

K*

Six miles north of Jerusalem on a high hill, once stood the city of Gibeon. This was one of the royal cities of Israel, as well as a city of refuge, but it is now only a small Arab village, containing nothing to show its former greatness. Through the village, and along the slope of the hill, are large piles of stone, the remains of ruined buildings, with here and there a relic of a temple, or palace, to mark the spot where once stood a royal city.

On the slope of the hill below the village is still to be seen the pool of Gibeon, which is so often referred to in the Bible, and where great events have occured, which are narrated therein. It was here at this pool, Joab and Abner met at the head of their respective armies of Judah, and Israel, and fought that memorable battle, in which many of the combatants of both armies were slain. Below the pool, lies the plain of Gibeon, which is also memorable for the past. This plain, although small, shows more fertility, and is better cultivated than any place that I have seen on these mountains. This is thought to be the place where Joshua attacked the Amorites, and on that account is visited by almost every person traveling through Palestine. The Bible says Joshua with his invading army marched from his camp at Gilgal, and attacked the Amorites, on the plains of Gibeon, and in order to complete his victory, he commanded the sun to stand still.

We next visited the ruins of Ai, which was located on a hill, as most all the ancient cities of Palestine were. This was the first city after Jericho, that Joshua took in his conquest of the Promised Land. Nothing now remains of this city, but heaps of stone scattered over the barren hill, without habitation, tree, shrub, or vegetation of any kind, or even one green thing on which the eye can rest.

Traveling north-east from here, we came to Ramah, the birthplace and residence of the prophet Jeremiah. Further on we came to Gilbah, spoken of in the Bible, as the largest city in the land of Benjamin, and the scene of a number of battles, in one of which the tribe of Benjamin was almost annihilated. This city was also the home of Saul, and seat of his government during the greater part of his reign. From Gilbah, we went north in the direction of Bethel. The country through which we passed is wild, barren and desolate, being a continuation of hill and dale, over rocky cliffs, and crossing dismal gorges. The inhabitants here are rough in appearance, and have a savage look. In some places they would collect around us in large numbers, demanding money for the privilege of traveling through their country. A Sheik of one of the villages offered to accompany us, and protect us from harm, if we would pay him ten shillings, but we declined his services.

This part of the country is said to be full of cut-throats and robbers, and some think it unsafe to travel through it without a guard, but no one attempted to molest us. Further than the annoyance of beggars, we had no difficulty.

While on these mountains, we fell in with a party of women and boys, who were engaged in collecting snails to sell in market. These snails are considered a great luxury by people here, and are served up at all the fashionable hotels in the Orient.

While on the Jerusalem and Galilee road, we met a caravan of Arab pilgrims from Damascus, and on their way to Mecca. In this caravan there were about fifty camels loaded with men, women, and children, while other camels were loaded with tents, provisions, etc. On the backs of some of these camels were placed large saddles, with a guard or railing around the top, so the whole family could sit around it, without being in danger of falling off.

In a village among the rocky defiles of the mountain, I saw many houses built against rocks, which form one side of the building, and in a few instances, families were living in grottos, which were cut out of the rocky cliff.

The sun was now getting low and our dragoman informed us that the gates of Jerusalem would be closed at dark, and there would be no admittance into the city after that time. We had many miles to ride over a rocky country, and the dragoman put his horse on a canter, and we followed after in Indian file, at a speed that was really frightful, but we reached the city in time to be admitted, and devoted the remainder of the evening to reflection on what we had seen among the mountains of Judea.

CHAPTER XXIV.

RETURN TO EUROPE.

On the fifth of December we bid a final adieu to Jeru-salem, and commenced our homeward tour, reaching Paris on the sixteenth day. At Joppa we boarded an Austrian steamer, running between Constantinople, and Alexandria. As the steamer weighed anchor and put to sea, we gave a long, farewell look at the Holy Land, a country alike dear to Christians, Jews, and Mahom-medans, the land of the patriarchs, prophets, and apostles.

The steamer was two days in her passage to Alexan-dria, distant by the way of Port Said, three hundred and twenty miles. Along the Egyptian coast for fifty miles, the water was muddied by the Nile, which was in striking contrast to the clear, blue water of the sea. In sailing down the coast, we had a fine view of Aboukir Bay, where in 1797, Lord Nelson destroyed the French fleet.

On arriving at Alexandria, I found a French steamer

about to sail for Marseilles, France. Hurrying to the shipping office, I bought a ticket for seventy dollars and succeeded in getting aboard while the ship was weighing anchor; but owing to the rough sea, she was unable to leave port until the next day.

The entrance to the harbor of Alexandria is both difficult and dangerous, and requires an experienced pilot to steer clear of rocks and sandbars. When the sea is rough, vessels will not attempt to enter, or leave port. At Alexandria, as well as other ports on the Mediterranean, no large vessels can approach the shore but are obliged to lie at anchor some distance off, and passengers and freight are carried back and forth in small boats.

Parting with my company at Alexandria, I found myself aboard of a steamer where no one could speak, or understand the English language, and during ten days which was occupied in making a passage of nearly two thousand miles, I was left to my own meditations. On this steamer, as well as other French vessels on which I have traveled, there are but two meals a day, break- fast at eleven, and dinner at six. These meals consist of a great variety of dishes on the table d'hote plan. Wine, and brandy are used as a part of the fare. After eating, an hour or more is spent at the table, drinking coffee, brandy, and smoking cigars. Notwithstanding the liquor was free to all, I never saw a person who appeared to be under its influence. On this steamer, frogs and snails were generally served up at dinner. The snails were large, and served up in the shell.

Those fond of snails would take their plate full of them and pull the snail out of its shell with a silver tong made for that purpose, when it is taken into the mouth, horns and all.

On this steamer was a fat, red-faced Dutchman, who was a steerage passenger, and like myself, found no one aboard of the ship, who could speak his language. This Dutchman had a great fondness for fishing, and he had prepared himself with a line the size of a bed cord, on the end of which, was a hook sufficiently large to hold a shark. The line was tied to the stern of the ship, and late and early, he was seen watching it, frequently drawing it in to examine the bait. One day while the Dutchman was at dinner, some mischievous fellows hauled in the line, and tied thereon an old pair of boots, and an old rug, weighing it down with a broken frying pan. The Dutchman soon discovered that he had caught something large, and news went over the steamer that a shark, or some other monstrous fish was caught, when everybody ran to the hurricane deck to see it. The Dutchman with hat and coat off, and sweat running down his face, commenced hawling in the line. We offered to assist him, but he refused all assistance preferring to retain all the honor and profit to himself. But when the prize was hauled on deck, he raised his hands in astonishment, scarcely crediting his own eyes, and showing the most woe-begone expression that I ever saw. But when he saw us laughing, he understood that a trick had been played on him, which put him into a terrible rage. With rapid jestures, he commenced yelling at the top of his voice, not one word of which we could understand, but supposed that he was blessing us.

When the weather is fair, a sail on the Mediterranean is very interesting, as the atmosphere is not so liable to fog, or mist, as on the Atlantic, and islands, and points of mainland can be seen at a great distance.

The European coast as far as I have seen, is mountainous, and destitute of timber, while the African, and Asiatic coast is flat. On this sea are frequently seen large shoals of flying fish, which at a distance look like a flock of white ducks. When the sea is rough, these fishes can only fly from wave to wave, but on a smooth sea, they will fly a long ways, occasionally dipping their wings into the water to wet them, then rise again. When the night is dark, phosphorous lights are seen by the side of the ship, sometimes of such brilliancy, as to appear like a continuous sheet of fire.

On our way we went close to the island of Candia, and followed its coast for more than one hundred miles, which gave us a fine view of its snow-capped mountains. Our next sight of land was the outlines of Mt. Ætna, although more than one hundred miles distant, was visible to the naked eye, and appeared like a great pyramid rising out of the sea. Passing the strait of Messina, with Sicily on one side, and Calabria on the other, we enjoyed a view of beautiful landscape scenery, probably not equalled on the Mediterranean. North of Sicily are located the Lipari Islands, consisting of a group of small islands, each of which contains a mountain. These islands with their mountains, look at a distance like huge hay stacks scattered over a level plain. Among this group of islands, is one called Tumberly, containing a volcano that is always in eruption, sending forth smoke, with flames of fire, and it is called the light house of the Mediterranean. Our ship passed this island after dark, and the light from its summit was so great, that a person could see to read on deck.

The direct course from the strait of Messina to Marseilles, lies between the islands of Sardinia and Corsica, but owing to the rough sea the captain was afraid to risk his ship near the rocky coast of these islands, and therefore went between them and the Italian coast. We passed close to the island of Elba, where Napolean was exiled. Farther up the coast, we had a fine view of Leghorn, and Genoa. It was after dark when we passed the cities of Nice and Toulon, and could see nothing but their beacon lights.

TOUR THROUGH FRANCE.

Marseilles is the most commercial city on the Mediterranean, and is the common center of trade for southern Europe. It has two harbors, an inner, and an outer one, both of which were full of ships. The new part of the city is well built, with many wide streets and high houses, and presents a constant hum of business.

L*

Two hundred and twenty miles north of Marseilles, in the valley of the Rhone is located the city of Lyons, containing nearly three hundred thousand inhabitants. This city is built on a hill, under a hill, and along the side of a hill, having narrow streets, and high houses. On every street, is heard the clicking of the silk looms. Lyons excels every other city in Europe, in the silk manufactories, and from that source, it has derived its wealth and importance.

On the road to Paris, and fifty-nine miles south of it, we came to the beautiful little city of Fontainebleau, a place identified with French history. The city contains a royal palace with beautiful flower gardens, among which are paved driveways, and is surrounded by a native forest of some miles in length, which belongs to the government of France. It was here Napoleon made his last defence against the allied forces, and from here he was exiled to Elba.

It is nearly six hundred miles from Marseilles to Paris, most of the way through a fine farming country, where the land is level and rich, and in which are many beautiful cities. In the southern part of France the fig and olive is cultivated, and here are extensive vineyards, as well as orchards of peaches, prunes, and apples. Having traveled through France in three different directions, and at different seasons of the year, gave me a good opportunity to see the country. These observations caused me to come to the conclusion that it is the best country in Europe, and is under the highest state of cultivation of any except England.

It was late in the afternoon when I arrived in Paris, and I told the hackman to drive me to my old quarters, the Grand Hotel d'Orleans, where I might see some familiar faces. Although eight months had elapsed since I left Paris, and my beard had grown during that time, to nearly a half foot in length, as soon as I entered the court of the hotel, I found myself surrounded by waiters, clerks, and proprietors, shaking me by the hand, with *Bon jour Monsieur Matson.*

Three months had elapsed since hearing from home, but on going to my bankers, I found a large package of letters awaiting me, some of which were from parties with whom I had traveled in my various rambles through Europe.

HOMEWARD BOUND.

After a stay of a few days in Paris, I continued my journey homeward, by way of Dieppe, and New Haven. On arriving in London, it appeared strange to hear everyone speaking English, after being eight months among people with whom I could not converse. Here I could communicate with everyone, and make all necessary inquiries; a pleasure that no person can appreciate, unless he has traveled in foreign countries. It was Christmas, and for three days, business places were closed, while the streets were full of well dressed people hurrying to and fro, enjoying the holidays. Here and there was heard the merry laugh of children at the reception of their Christmas presents. But it was not so in some of the poorer districts of London, where people are dependant on each day's labor, and the suspension of business even for a few days, leaves many to starve.

Taking a cab, I made a visit to Shadwell, .a noted place in the eastern part of the city. Here poverty, ignorance, and vice reigns supreme, exceeding anything I have ever met before. No toy shops are seen here to gladden the hearts of the little ones, but at one corner of almost every street, there is a dirty beer shop, while on the opposite corner, is its principle support and mainstay, a pawnbrokers office. The half naked children playing in the dirty streets were evidently unconscious that it was a day of pleasure and universal merry-making. At the corners of dark, narrow streets, groups of gloomy looking men were seen standing; not conversing with each other, but waiting in expectation that some one would pass in search of laborers. Here haggard looking women, with tattered dresses, and in some cases barefooted, were seen passing through the streets, begging from each passer-by.

On some of the doors, bills were posted, offering to lodge persons for two pence per night. This place has the appearance of decay; many of the shops were closed, and the words, " To let," appear on almost every house. In the worst part of this miserable locality I was surprised to come suddenly upon four large blocks of imposing buildings, known as Peabody Square These buildings were erected by Mr. Peabody, the American banker, for the benefit of the poor, where they can obtain apartments at a lower rate than elsewhere, and the unfortunate tenant will not be turned out of doors, at the first failure to pay the rent.

In London a person will be surprised at the shortness of the days in mid-winter, and to me having made a sudden transit from the south it was more apparent. In dull weather, the city is mostly enveloped in fog or smoke, sometimes both, which makes it difficult to do business before ten o'clock in the morning, and gas is frequently lighted at two o'clock in the afternoon.

Early in the morning of the thirty-first inst., I left London for Liverpool, two hundred and two miles distant. The train moved with that velocity peculiar to the English express, which is unequaled in any other part of the world. Soon the great metropolis of the world faded in the distance, its locality only being marked by the dense cloud of black smoke, which ever hovers over this abode of wealth, poverty, and crime. The first place of interest on the road was Oxford, which is famous for its institutions of learning. The next was Warwick containing the old castle where once lived the celebrated Earl of Warwick, who is called by historians the king maker. Farther on we crossed the river Avon, near the city of Stratford, the native place of Shakespeare. Then through Birmingham, a large manufacturing city containing three hundred thousand inhabitants, and called the toy shop of Europe. At last the black, smoky city of Liverpool was reached, and my travels in the east were at an end, as I sailed the next day, in the steam ship Cuba, for New York.

CROSSING THE ATLANTIC.

Twenty-four hours sail on the Irish Sea, brought us to Queenstown, where we took on a few passengers, and eighty-four bags of mail, and again put to sea. Soon the outlines of the Irish coast faded in the distance, and we bade farewell to Europe. On the second day out from Queenstown, a terrible gale arose, which continued for three days, causing much sea sickness among the passengers. At each plunge of the vessel into the foaming billows, she would ship tons of water, which would roll off her decks as she rose on the swells, only to go down again as before. All communication with the deck was closed, and during the long winter nights, the bells of the watch, and the hoarse notes of the speaking trumpet conveying orders to different parts of the ship could be heard above the roaring of wind and waves. Most of the passengers kept their state rooms on account of sea sickness, and the large dining hall was almost deserted. At one time only four of us answered to the summons of the steward's call.

On the fourth day the wind abated, when people came on deck to look out for whales and sharks, and to amuse themselves in watching the antics of sea gulls, and mother Carry's chickens. Large flocks of the former followed the ship across the Atlantic, to pick up crumbs thrown from the table. Each day a reckoning was made, showing the latitude, and longitude of the ship, and the clock was changed to the true time.

One day it was announced at the cabin door, that a whale was in sight, when we all ran to the hurricane deck to see the monster, but were disappointed to find it about three miles off, so that we could only see its spouting.   While looking at the water thrown up by his whaleship, another whale appeared much closer, and we could see his huge body every time he came up to spout.

On the thirteenth day out, we had a complete calm, when the great Atlantic became perfectly smooth, and enveloped in fog, which required the ringing of the bell once a minute, through the day, to prevent collision with other vessels.   One hundred miles from New York, we took on board a pilot to conduct us into port.   This pilot had been ten days at sea in a pilot yacht, looking for a job.   He had with him a large bundle of dailies which were eagerly sought for, although ten days old.

On the fifteenth day from Liverpool, we landed in New York, when the ship was besieged by a regiment of custom house officers, and my baggage underwent an examination for the thirty-seventh time since I left home.